This book belongs to

_____

_____

NORTH STAR BOOKS

LOUISA MAY
ALCOTT

NORTH STAR BOOKS

LOUISA MAY ALCOTT

HELEN WAITE PAPASHVILY

Illustrated by Bea Holmes

1965

HOUGHTON MIFFLIN COMPANY BOSTON
The Riverside Press Cambridge

ANOTHER PROFILE IN COURAGE

Louisa May Alcott, best known for her beloved LITTLE
WOMEN, *belongs in any pantheon of courageous American
women. Like Jo in her fictionized biography of the always
idealistic, always poor Alcott family, Louisa had an indom-
itable spirit no matter how great the odds against her.*

*She was a staunch defender of her father, Bronson Alcott,
who kept his head in the stars, but seldom had his feet on the
ground. If he wished to give away all the food in the house
or the winter's firewood, or take the family on a feather-
brained mission to live in a communal colony, Louisa was
behind him every step of the way.*

*How she managed to rise from poverty through teaching
herself to be one of America's best-selling writers, and how
she carried, as part of her willing load, the entire dependent
family, becomes an American classic in this excellent biography by an equally courageous woman, Helen Papashvily.*

*Girls of today who think they have problems will be sur-
prised to discover that their little difficulties seldom compare
to the militant struggle which faced most women of the previous century. It gives us all courage to read a book such as
this one.*

STERLING NORTH
General Editor

For
Percy and Amy Ruhe
and all those who were once
Little Men and Little Women
at the Ruhest

CONTENTS

1

Boston

1838

"LITTLE GIRL lost! Little girl lost!"

Through the narrow cobblestoned streets of Boston the town crier went, by turns clanging his bell and calling.

"Little girl lost! Little girl lost! Six years old. In a pink dress — white hat — green shoes — Little girl lost!"

No one had seen her. Not the housemaid polishing the panes of an upper window; not the children jumping rope on the pavement, not the fine ladies in their hooped skirts and plumed bonnets out for an afternoon stroll.

The crier tried one street after another.

"Little girl lost. LOST!"

The clock in a church steeple struck four, five, and then six. The crier turned toward the Common, fifty acres of countryside set down in the heart of the city. Its wide fields where children played in the daytime looked deserted now, but the crossing walks were crowded with men homeward bound from work. More than one paused and listened with a sad shake of his head to the crier.

Boston was no longer a village where everyone knew his neighbor, but, in this year of 1838, a bustling town of 60,000 people, a perilous place for a six-year-old wandering all alone. The crier, thinking of runaway horses, open wharfs, gypsies, flash fires, and the angry mobs that sometimes roamed the streets, shook his head too, and walked a little faster and called a little louder.

When he reached the edge of the Common he stopped, found a horehound drop in his pocket and popped it into his mouth. Where, oh where would the wanderer be most likely to go? Winter Street? Summer Street? Temple Place? The crier sighed. Guessing was useless. Block by block, he must keep on until he covered the whole town. He swallowed his lozenge, cleared his throat, gave his bell a shine or two on his sleeve, and started off again.

"Little girl lost . . ." It was long past seven o'clock and dark when the crier turned into Bedford Street, still calling, "Lost. Lost. Little girl . . ."

A great Newfoundland lying on a doorstep raised his head and tipped his ears at the noise.

". . . in a pink dress . . . white hat . . . new green shoes. LOST . . ."

A child fast asleep beside the dog, her head on his curly back, awoke too, and listened.

"Why, that's me," she cried.

The crier stopped and looked down. By the light

of the street lamp he saw, smiling up at him, a very pretty child with dark eyes, a warm olive complexion, and a mass of long brown hair.

"Are you Mr. Bronson Alcott's daughter, Louisa May?" he asked.

She nodded her head happily.

The crier was puzzled. The lost children he found were always tearstained and dirty and they screamed between sobs and hiccoughs to be taken home. This one was different. She seemed to be enjoying her adventure, and she was quite unwilling to part with her new friend, the big dog.

Finally the crier picked her up and carried her home to her anxious parents, who gave her some supper

and put her to bed. Long after she was asleep, her father and mother pondered, as they had so often before, why of their three daughters it was always Louisa May who fell into mischief.

Her sister Anna, not quite two years older, was dependable and considerate, and, instead of wandering away, helped her mother cook and sew and care for Elizabeth, the baby of the family. Even little Beth, as she was called, although only four, was gentle and obedient. Louisa was the difficult one.

"What," her despairing mother often had cause to ask, "makes her so willful?"

"Hers is the wild exuberance of a powerful nature," Mr. Alcott would remind his wife. "Anna bears and forebears to gain strength, growth, and life. Louisa wrestles with obstacles and learns by contention."

Bronson Alcott was an unusually gifted man, a teacher and a philosopher, with many original ideas about the development of children. Although his daughter, Louisa May, often challenged, and more than once upset his careful theories, she had a very special place in his heart from the day she was born on his thirty-third birthday, November 29, 1832, in Germantown, Pennsylvania.

Mr. Alcott, a New Englander, had been invited to this little Quaker village near Philadelphia to establish a private school. The venture did not prosper, and when Louisa was two it was decided to return to

Boston, Mrs. Alcott's old home.

Their books and furniture packed, their farewells said, the family embarked on a coastal vessel in the Delaware River. The other passengers must have watched with interest as the Alcotts came aboard, for their distinguished manner and appearance commanded attention in any company.

Mrs. Alcott, an erect, handsome woman with dark eyes and a mass of chestnut curls, walked with Anna, a plump, fair, sunny-faced, four-year-old. After them, taking giant strides with his long legs, came Mr. Alcott, his pale golden hair blowing in the breeze. Seldom impatient, almost never angry, his bright blue eyes and gentle smile reflected a serene yet determined nature. On her father's shoulder rode Louisa, then not quite two, and, according to a family friend, ". . . a dear, little pet, pretty in an uncommon degree . . . with dark bright eyes, long dark hair and countenance of more than usual intelligence . . ."

When all the passengers were on board, the whistle blew, the sailors cast off the lines, and the ship nosed down the river. Scarcely had the voyage begun before an alarm sounded for a missing child. A little girl just learning to walk, dressed in a new nankeen frock had disappeared. Could she have fallen overboard? Crew and passengers searched frantically, until a sailor found a dirty ragamuffin down in the engine room. It was, under several layers of grease, Louisa May.

Now, four years later, Louisa May was more adventurous than ever. Curious and fearless, she roamed Boston Common with its meadows, uplands, and rocky glens. She and Anna played hide-and-find, darting between the great elms and oaks and crouching in the clumps of spruce. Sometimes they visited the zoo in one corner of the Common and fed apples to the animals, although it always made Beth sad because the eagle had to live in a cage. At Frog Pond the girls watched ice skaters in winter and boys sailing boats in summer. Once, Louisa, dabbling at the water's edge, slipped and fell in. She nearly drowned before a Negro boy pulled her out. All three of the girls had hoops they rolled along the Common's cross-walks. Louisa drove hers with such speed and skill that even the boys stopped to watch her.

The Common provided continuous entertainment. The girls could see soldiers drilling and the horse troops, a red pennant streaming from every pointed lance, go parading by. Once, on a crisp, never-to-be-forgotten fall afternoon, a band of Sioux and Iowa Indians visited Boston and camped on the Common. They wore horned bonnets, robes of wild animal skins, and brandished terrible weapons as they stamped through a mock war dance. Beth was frightened and cried to go home. Anna did not like the spectacle either.

"I'm glad it's a sham battle," she said. "Real battles must be cruel and bloody." She led Beth away.

But Louisa stayed and watched as long as the screaming, stamping Indians performed.

She often lingered long after her sisters had gone home. She liked to play on the ash heaps with poor Irish children. Sometimes she went home with them and shared their supper of cold potatoes, salt fish, and breadcrusts.

When the Common was quiet Louisa explored the busy streets of the city. She watched the blacksmith, drenched in a shower of golden sparks, shoe a horse. She stopped at the organ factory, and sometimes stole a breathless, downhill ride in the delivery cart. She strolled along India Wharf, sniffing the pungent cargoes of ships home from the Orient — camphorwood, ginger, coffee. Someday, Louisa decided, she would go to the faraway places where these things grew. She would visit Africa too, and see the elephants and lions and travel through Europe and climb the Alps to the very top and bring home presents — books for her father, a French doll for Beth . . . So Louisa dreamed on until her parents or some of their friends came searching for her.

Once, a long, long way from home she met her Grandfather May. Handsome and distinguished, he was the last man in Boston to dress in the old colonial style with knee breeches, cocked hat, and buckles on his shoes. This grandchild who bore his name delighted him. Instead of scolding, he took her into a pastry shop, bought her gingerbread, and carried her home to be forgiven.

Louisa, of course, did not always go unpunished. The day after the crier found her with the Newfoundland, her mother tied her to the arm of a chair in the parlor to meditate for an hour or two on all the trouble and anxiety she had caused by her thoughtless behavior. A very few times, for deliberate disobedience or for striking Anna, Louisa was spanked. But usually Mr. Alcott, who believed kindness was the best disci-

pline, talked to Louisa seriously, appealing to her con-
science and reason. Perhaps he, always gentle and
calm himself, best understood her tempestuous nature.

Like her mother, Louisa had boundless energy and
a quick tongue and temper, but she also shared her
father's deep compassion for all living things, his
idealism and his profound sincerity.

Mr. Alcott knew from careful observation that
Louisa was a creature of contradictions. Both practical
and imaginative, daring yet shy, she could be stubborn and proud one minute, sweet and generous the
next. While she might stamp her feet in a tantrum at
bedtime, she could, nevertheless, appear at the breakfast table next morning exclaiming, "I love everybody
in this whole wide world."

When Louisa was six she began to attend her father's
classes. Mr. Alcott was an unusual teacher with an
unusual school. Few children in those days had any
chance for a real education. For three or four "terms,"
perhaps a year in all, they sat on backless benches in
dark, dreary, dirty rooms parroting in unison, "c-a-t,
cat; h-a-t, hat." They wrote with squealing pencils on
slates, memorized, repeated, and learned to keep quiet.

There might be a few tattered books in the schoolroom, perhaps a wall map, dulled by smoke and grease,
and for the slow learners a stool and a peaked dunce
cap. The only thing sure to be new and in good sup-

ply were the switches or rulers, for parents and teachers alike felt sure that education must be pounded into children.

Mr. Alcott, almost alone in his time, disagreed. He thought learning should be an exciting, happy adventure. After his return to Boston from Philadelphia, he started Temple School to carry out his ideas.

Beautiful surroundings, he believed, encouraged study, so he rented two spacious rooms in the Masonic Temple Building in the center of Boston. The furniture and equipment he selected were expensive, and since his funds were low he bought everything on credit. Mrs. Alcott worried about this debt, but her husband, confident that his school would succeed, assured her he could soon pay all he owed.

Mr. Alcott made Temple School a pleasant place. Each child had a comfortable desk, a chair, and a little blackboard. Sun streamed in through the tall windows on a bright carpet; there were pictures, sculpture, a globe, growing plants, and shelves full of fresh books.

Mr. Alcott taught so that children would understand and remember. For Louisa and the other beginners he made the letters of the alphabet — not on paper with a pencil — but on the floor with himself.

"See, children," he stretched out flat, his arms close to his sides, his long legs apart, ". . . this is the shape of Y!"

Up again, he held his arms out straight from his sides, ". . . T!" He arched thumbs and forefingers together in a circle, ". . . O."

Almost before she knew it Louisa was reading.

The more advanced pupils had geography, mathematics, music, reading, and Latin. Mr. Alcott used stories and parables to explain difficult points. He did his best to help all his pupils develop self-discipline, moral judgment, and social responsibility. Since he was always kind and courteous, he expected the class to be attentive and well-behaved. If, while reading aloud, he heard whispering, he never scolded, he simply put the book down and waited until it was quiet again before going on. When one or two misbehaved, he pointed out, the entire community suffered by it. He only punished a pupil if the whole room, including the culprit himself, agreed it was deserved.

Parents had never heard of such a thing. "Does Mr. Alcott know what he's doing?" they asked each other.

"His own daughters aren't perfect." So the gossip went.

"Louisa May has a temper."

"She and her sisters wander all over the Common."

"Spare the rod and spoil the child!"

Several families transferred their children to old-fashioned schools and stricter discipline.

Mr. Alcott saw no reason to change his methods. His school was orderly and the students were progressing rapidly. Each morning he gathered them in a circle around him for a period of conversation. He welcomed their questions and ideas, for children, he believed, possessed a certain instinctive knowledge of truth that adults often lost. Anna and Louisa found nothing strange in this. Their father always paid careful attention to their opinions. He even listened to little Beth's prattle. In the same way he encouraged his students to talk of themselves, of their understanding of the soul and the body, of right and wrong, of this world and the next.

Old Bostonians found this more shocking than his

discipline. Didn't the proverb say, "Children should be seen but not heard?" Several more pupils were removed from his school. No new ones enrolled.

Mr. Alcott, sure he was right, kept cheerfully on. Fewer students meant less money, he explained to his daughters. Beth was too small to understand, but Anna and Louisa knew they must do without new toys and dresses and books.

They moved from their comfortable house in Front Street to a smaller one in Cottage Place. Some of their furniture had to be sold. The girls could see that their mother was worried. Mr. Alcott stayed as serene and confident as ever. He was busy writing a book about his conversations with his pupils. Once his critics understood his methods, Mr. Alcott felt sure that their attacks on his school would cease.

Louisa liked to be near her father while he worked. She pushed her toys down the stairs and into his study. A coal fire burned in the grate. The curtains were drawn; the lamp glowed. The room was quiet except for the tick, tick, tick of the clock and the scratch of Mr. Alcott's quill pen. Louisa watched him fill page after page with his flowing script. She often made up stories for Beth and Anna. Perhaps she could write down her "plays," as she called them, and make a book, too, someday.

Anna crept in with her toys. They played quietly together before the hearth for a time. Then Louisa picked up Anna's doll. Anna snatched it away. They quarreled and Louisa, enraged, picked up the poker and threatened her sister. Mr. Alcott stopped his work, spoke sternly to Louisa, and sent her from the room. Anna, always forgiving, went after her and they soon made friends again.

Sometimes Beth played in the study with them. Once she fell asleep on the floor and Anna and Louisa built a house around her of the largest books. Then they went on an errand and stopped to play on the Common and forgot all about their prisoner. When Beth awoke, she screamed until her father came to her rescue.

At last, despite these and many similar interruptions, Mr. Alcott finished his manuscript and sent it off to the publisher. It was a proud moment for the whole family when the first copies, neatly printed and bound, appeared in the bookseller's window. Anna could spell out the long title — *Conversations with Children on the Gospels.*

Their joy was short-lived. Contrary to Mr. Alcott's hopes, the book did not silence his old critics but instead stirred up new trouble. People were horrified when they read that Mr. Alcott had discussed God, Christ, birth, life, and death with children.

"What can the young know of such subjects," clergymen thundered from their pulpits. Newspapers and magazines attacked Mr. Alcott more sharply than ever

before. Rumors, accusations, and falsehoods about
Temple School flew through the town. Old acquaint-
ances crossed the street to avoid meeting Mr. Alcott.

Many friends, however, did remain loyal. Temple
School in its short existence had won favorable notice
from progressive educators at home and abroad. Some
of the most brilliant men in New England came to
Mr. Alcott's defense. Chief among them, perhaps, was
Ralph Waldo Emerson, a philosopher of world re-
nown who wrote and spoke in favor of Mr. Alcott,
his school, and his book. He was a tall, quiet man
whose reserve and dignity awed grown people, but

Louisa and her sisters found him patient and understanding.

William Russell, the first editor of the *American Journal of Education,* was another of Mr. Alcott's staunch supporters. The Russell children were favorite playmates of the Alcott girls.

Miss Elizabeth Peabody, who once taught at Temple School and lived for a few months with the Alcotts, came to visit them too. Her bonnet and dress were often askew, and she was so absentminded she bumped into trees and then apologized to them, but she spoke six languages and had the respect of scholars all over the world. She smelled of peppermints and she usually found a bagful in her skirt pocket for Beth, her namesake, to share with her sisters.

Although it seemed hopeless to change the public's opinion of Mr. Alcott, these and many other friends tried, each in his own way, to help. Meantime Mr. Alcott's courage and determination never faltered. Although only a handful of students remained, he continued his school unchanged.

"Tomorrow I expect a new pupil," Mr. Alcott announced one evening. "A little girl. Our friend William Russell asked me to take her."

Mrs. Alcott's face brightened. Perhaps better times were ahead for the school after all.

"What's her name, Father?" Anna asked.

"Susan Robinson."

"Is she as big as I am?" Louisa wanted to know. "Can she read?"

"She is older than either you or Anna. She cannot read because she has never had a chance to learn. Susan is a Negro."

"A slave?" Anna asked.

"No, Susan is free. She must have an education if she is to help herself and her race."

"She can use my slate," Louisa promised, "and my books."

"I wish all the colored people were free," Anna sighed.

She and Louisa knew about slavery and the suffering and oppression of the Negro people. Their uncle Samuel May had worked long and hard for the abolition of slavery, and their father's friend Mr. William Lloyd Garrison was the editor of *The Liberator*, the leading anti-slavery newspaper.

Mr. and Mrs. Alcott believed all Negroes should be free. Sometimes they hid runaway slaves in the house. Once Louisa discovered a Negro in the big outdoor bake oven. Startled, but not afraid, she told her father. Mr. Alcott explained that the man had escaped from his master and was trying to reach Canada where slavery was illegal. She must tell no one, he warned her.

Louisa kept the secret. She remembered with a grateful heart that it was a colored boy who had saved her from drowning in Frog Pond. She welcomed Susan Robinson heartily when she came to school with Elizabeth and Mary Russell. The other pupils soon made friends with the newcomer, and for a few happy days all went well. Then the storm broke.

"Awful! Terrible! Have you heard?" Again the town buzzed with gossip.

"This time Mr. Alcott has gone too far!"

"Teach a Negro child to read and write! Let her learn with white children! Unbelievable!"

Angry, frightened and most of all confused, the parents of the few remaining students descended on Mr. Alcott.

"Dismiss Susan Robinson," they insisted.

Mr. Alcott listened to their blustering demands with his usual dignity. Then, in courteous tones, he explained that he had accepted Susan Robinson as a pupil. She was diligent and well-behaved. He saw no reason, therefore, to send her away.

"Then my Lucia goes," one parent shouted.

"And my Charles," another spoke out.

"And Andrew and Edward."

"And William."

One by one, Louisa saw her friends empty their desks and depart, often without being allowed to say goodbye.

Now the town was really aroused. The ignorant, the prejudiced, and the malicious joined forces to attack

Mr. Alcott. He was ridiculed and condemned. Rowdies jeered as he walked through the streets.

Mrs. Alcott pleaded with him to stay at home. Boston mobs were notoriously dangerous and violent, prone to destroy whatever they could not understand.

They had dragged William Lloyd Garrison through the streets with a halter around his neck, and nearly killed George Thompson, another friend of the Alcotts, for lecturing against slavery. Mr. Alcott might be the next one to suffer, perhaps die, for his principles.

He ignored the danger, however, and continued his daily trip to school. Louisa and Anna, walking by his side, learned to ignore the stares and sneers of the street-corner idlers. Sometimes they heard muttering and catcalls, too, as they passed and it was always a relief when they reached the school.

Although only Louisa and Anna, the Russells, and Susan Robinson were left, they continued having lessons as usual, until one day they were interrupted by a loud knock on the door. A man entered.

"Mr. Alcott."

Louisa saw her father's quiet nod.

"I'm the City Marshall. I've come to collect the money you owe on this furniture for your school. Can you pay?"

Mr. Alcott shook his head sadly.

"Your creditors want their money."

"I know," Mr. Alcott said, "but I can't —"

"Then I must take the furniture back."

"If you could wait — " Mr. Alcott said.

"Can't. My orders are the money or the furnishings."
He picked up the globe and the statue of Shakespeare.
"My men will be up for the rest."

As Anna and Louisa watched the maps, the pictures,
the carefully chosen library, the pretty desks, the
bright curtains were carried away.

Mr. Alcott, his dream dismantled before his eyes, at
last gave up and sat with bowed head and broken
heart in his empty schoolroom.

Bewildered, the children looked at each other. Finally Anna touched his shoulder. "Father!"

For once Mr. Alcott did not respond to the gentle
voice.

"Father," Louisa spoke, "we must go home now."
She tugged at his sleeve.

He rose, put on his cloak, and the three walked
wordlessly back to Cottage Place.

Mrs. Alcott, after one quick glance, put her husband
to bed and called her brother-in-law Dr. Windship.

Mr. Alcott was ill, so ill that he did not care what
happened; he did not even know that one night a stone
came crashing through their window. But Louisa,
crouching by the fire in the dark study, heard the shat-
tering glass and the dull thud. Had the mob come for
her father? Would they break down the doors? Drag

him away? Furious and unafraid, she ran to the front
door and threw it open.

"Go away, go away," she shouted into the dark
street. "Go away, bad men, and let my father alone!"

FOR NEARLY two months Mr. Alcott kept to his room. Louisa and Anna tiptoed through the house helping their mother care for the invalid. During this time the excitement over Temple School gradually subsided, and the mob found new victims to harass. The gossips, however, kept up their attack. Neither Louisa nor anyone else could silence *them*.

Perhaps a less dedicated man than Mr. Alcott might have explained or apologized, and, in so doing, managed to keep his school. To him, compromise in matters of principle bordered on dishonesty. Whether he was right or wrong in this instance, one thing was certain — his career as a professional educator seemed to be at an end. His publisher sold the remaining copies of his book for waste paper. Mr. Alcott had no income, no prospects, no plans for the future.

Relatives rallied to the Alcotts' aid. Mrs. Alcott's father, Colonel May, and Dr. Windship came often, and her brother, the Reverend Samuel May, drove in from Scituate on the shore where he served as a minister of the Unitarian church.

Friends called. Almost every day Anna or Louisa

opened the door to some distinguished visitor. It might be Mr. Emerson or Professor Charles Follen from Harvard University, or Washington Allston, the poet-painter, or the Reverend Theodore Parker.

The Reverend Theodore Parker was famous for his learning, eloquence, and prodigious strength. As a boy on his father's farm, he once told the Alcott girls, he helped clear the fields of huge granite boulders and, all by himself, he could lift and carry a barrel full of cider. His usual load, however, when he came to the Alcotts', was a stack of books from his enormous library to share with his sick friend.

When the doctor thought that Mr. Alcott was well enough to travel, the family left Boston and went to Scituate, where Samuel May had found them a house for the summer. As long as she lived Louisa never forgot the wonder and joy of those weeks she spent beside the ocean. Standing by the door of their wind-swept cottage, she watched the gulls wheeling and dipping, tasted the salt spray on her lips, and caught the tang of the cove — a pungent mixture of wet nets, dried fish, hot pitch, and ripening beach plums. From waking to sleeping she heard the crashing rhythm of the sea breaking on the rocks.

The whole family rose at dawn. In the early, fog-draped hours of the new day, even the most common-place chores — washing dishes, sweeping floors, and making beds — seemed mysterious. As soon as the

sun broke through the mist the girls dashed to the beach to see what new treasures the ocean offered. Shells, polished pebbles, driftwood, and delicate sea plants littered the sand. Each wave, with reckless generosity, cast a fresh assortment at their feet. When they found odd bits of flotsam, a triangle of ruby glass, a strange seed pod, or perhaps a cork float, Louisa would make up stories to explain how and why they came here.

The Alcotts went wading and swimming with their three May cousins and their friends. The beach was gay with boys and girls in bathing costumes of red and blue flannel. It was a question which the children enjoyed most — their own dip in the water or watching the adults venture in. Swimming in the ocean was such a daring new fad that no one had a real bathing suit. Neat ladies and dignified gentlemen disappeared into the dressing rooms and out came queer, short-skirted women with flop-brimmed hats and barefooted men in cut-down pantaloons. It made Louisa laugh to see these strange creatures skipping over the sand and jumping up and down in the water.

When the surf grew too rough to bathe, Louisa and her sisters spent hours at what they called "plays," pretending to be fine ladies or vegetable sellers or travelers in a coach. The girls made up the plot and action suited to the particular role as they went along. When they tired of their old "plays," Louisa invented new ones.

"Let's be poor beggars. In ragged clothes. Starving."

If Anna looked doubtful, Louisa was always ready with another idea.

"Then lords and nobles? With swords and steeds?"

This sounded too warlike for gentle Beth.

"I know. Queens at a ball?" Louisa's imagination never failed.

"To be queens at a ball we should really have dresses with long trains," Anna said.

"We will," Louisa promised. She could make royal

robes out of an old curtain and turn a gilt-paper button card into a crown.

Although it was summer, the girls had lessons every day with their father, and their mother taught them sewing — how to hem, darn, and mend. Louisa learned to tat, and she started to embroider a pair of slippers, but she made little progress. Long afterward she remembered that every time she threaded her needle it seemed as if she glimpsed some of the boys racing about "as full of tricks as circus tumblers," and she ran off to join them, her sewing forgotten.

On Sundays the Alcotts attended Uncle Samuel's church. Often, after the service, the whole congregation picnicked in a nearby grove. Unpacking great hampers, the ladies spread the tables with cakes and pies of every description. There were melons, clusters of raisins, bowls of peaches in rich cream. After the feast, sitting in the shade of the trees, they all sang hymns together. Louisa wished they might stay in Scituate forever.

All too soon September came. The summer visitors closed their houses and went back to town. It was too cold to bathe in the ocean any more. The days grew shorter. Grandfather May arrived from Boston for the last visit of the season. The Alcotts and Uncle Samuel's family all crowded into the parlor in the evening for conversation, games, and music. After Colonel May sang the old ballads he loved, "Woodlawn Hollow"

and "The Vicar of Bray," his deep bass filling the room, the children would beg him to tell what they called his "queer" stories — tales of hobgoblins, sprites, and haunted houses.

"Once on a stormy night," he might begin, "a lonely traveler came to a deserted inn . . ." As he went on, he made the wind howl, chains clank, doors creak. His gift for mimicry, his dramatic delivery, charmed Louisa. She would sit listening until her head drooped, her eyes closed, and she fell asleep on the floor.

In October the Alcotts went back to Boston. Mr. Alcott tried to find a teaching position. No one would hire him. He tried to write. No one would print his manuscripts.

The Russells and Susan still came for lessons with Mr. Alcott. Beth, too, joined her sisters in the classroom. Louisa was proving a good student. She learned to print clearly with a pencil, and she read everything she could find — poetry, fairy tales, and adventure stories. *Robinson Crusoe* and *Pilgrim's Progress* were great favorites. This latter Louisa and Anna liked so well that it became one of their plays. With a staff in hand, a ragbag for a pack, they were two "pilgrims" making their "progress" upstairs and down until they reached their "Celestial City" in the attic.

On November 29, 1839, Louisa was seven-years-old and Mr. Alcott forty. It was a happy day. Louisa always felt proud to share her birthday with her beloved father. When she awoke she found presents beside her bed — a pincushion, books, and from her mother, a new doll in a pink calico dress and sunbonnet. With it was a letter:

My Dear Little Girl, Will you accept this doll from me on your seventh birthday? She will be a quiet playmate for my active Louisa for seven years more. Be a kind Mama, and love her for my sake.

Your Mother

A few weeks before, her Grandfather had given her a diary. Her mother and father and Anna each kept a daily journal. Now Louisa, too, could set down her thoughts and impressions, her hopes and resolutions.

In the weeks that followed her birthday, however, there was nothing very cheerful for her to record. Soon after Temple School failed, the Alcotts had given up their comfortable house on Front Street for a smaller one in Cottage Place. Now they were forced to move again to a cold and dreary house. The girls shivered as they sat trying to do their lessons. There was no money to buy coal, scarcely enough, indeed, for food. They had wheat porridge for breakfast, vegetables and boiled rice for dinner. It seemed to Louisa that she was always hungry.

Mr. Alcott did not eat meat, and he discouraged,

although he did not forbid, its use by his family.

When he said, "Cruelty stares at me from the butcher's face; the deathset eyes of beasts peer at me and accuse me of belonging to a race of murderers," the girls did not feel like eating a piece of beef.

Carrots and squash and potatoes might satisfy Anna, and a bowl of bread and milk do for Beth, but Louisa wanted something more. Coming in one day after a long run on the Common, she looked in the cupboard and found just a single apple. She took it, put it back, picked it up again. Although she felt guilty, she was so hungry she could not resist taking one bite, and another, and another. At last, with only the core in her hand, she found her father in his study and confessed what she had done.

Gravely her father explained that the apple belonged to the whole family, and for her to take it for herself without permission was wrong.

"Was it — was it the same as — as stealing, Father?"

"Yes, my child."

"Even if it was only an apple?"

To take anything, no matter how small, that belongs to another is stealing, Mr. Alcott told her.

"I won't do it again," Louisa said.

Her heart was heavy. She knew she had disappointed her father. She wanted to be good; she tried to be good — but something always interfered.

This time, however, she was able to keep her promise. She was not tempted to take apples again because some delicious treats came her way. By a happy chance Anna and Louisa were sent on an errand one day to an old family friend who lived at the United States Hotel. They arrived just as she was finishing her dinner. The waiter, after whisking away the remains, reappeared with a silver dish.

"Dessert, Madam? Our chef's triumph."

"Not this evening. Thank you."

Anna and Louisa turned their eyes away as the waiter started back to the kitchen with a spun sugar dove on a nest of cream pudding.

"Wait a moment," their friend said. "On second thought, you may leave my dessert."

The sugar bird flew back to the table.

As soon as the door was closed, she whispered to the girls, "Will you eat it for me? To help me out?" She handed each of them a spoon.

The pudding was delicious — as delicious as anything unshared with their father and mother and Baby Beth could be.

"Will you do me a great favor?" their friend asked, when they had finished.

Anna and Louisa nodded.

"I'm served far more here than I can eat, and yet the cook is hurt if I send it back. You often take a little walk about this time of day?"

"Yes." Anna and Louisa spoke together.

"Then perhaps you might stop here and 'remove' my dessert to your house?"

"Oh, yes."

After that the girls called frequently at the hotel. Somewhere Louisa found a stylish hatbox to carry along. It always came out heavier than it went in, with perhaps a frosted cake, some slices of fresh pineapple, a mocha pudding, a few cherry tarts, or another sugar bird safely packed inside.

These treats supplemented the Alcott's sparse meals, but there were still clothes, candles, and shoes to be

bought and the rent to pay. The family moved again to a cheaper house on Beach Street.

Although the neighborhood was poor and the rooms small, a brilliant circle of men and women still gathered at the Alcotts'. Mr. and Mrs. Emerson came, and brought their friend Margaret Fuller, a writer and lecturer. Louisa thought she looked like a swan with her arching neck and inquisitive glance. Miss Peabody and her sister Mary were frequent visitors, and so was William Lloyd Garrison, editor of *The Liberator*, an abolitionist newspaper. Slave owners feared his fire and fury, but to the Alcott girls he was always gentle and affectionate.

These and many other people enjoyed Mr. Alcott's "Conversations," half lecture and half discussion, usually on some philosophic topic. His simplicity of manner, sincerity of purpose, originality of mind, charmed his audiences. "Listening to him," said one lady, "is like going to heaven in a rocking chair." Ralph Waldo Emerson thought his friend Alcott ". . . fit to talk with Plato."

Louisa and Anna were too young to join the company who sat in the little parlor, tossing ideas back and forth like so many bouncing balls. Nevertheless, the girls had an important share in the success of these occasions. Mrs. Alcott possessed a real gift for creating an atmosphere of comfort and charm. She taught her girls that cleanliness and order as much as color and design bring beauty to a room, however small and plain.

Anna and Louisa, with help from little Beth, swept the floor, polished the fire brass, rubbed the old mahogany furniture to satin smoothness with beeswax and arranged each piece to the best advantage. For the Alcotts pictures, sculpture, books, and flowers made the richest ornaments. The girls put scattered volumes in the library in order, straightened the bust of Socrates, dusted his classic nose, and arranged bunches of bayberry in the vases. They helped receive the guests and later passed the simple refreshments.

From time to time Mr. Alcott received invitations to give one of his Conversations in a neighboring town. Public speakers were popular entertainers, able, if they were shrewd, to command good fees. Mr. Alcott, unfortunately, could not bargain. He gave his best to every audience, always confident he would receive a like return. Consequently, he often trudged home, tired and spent, with little or nothing in his pocket.

Bills mounted. Louisa and Anna opened the door to a stream of shopkeepers and tradesmen who asked to see Mr. Alcott "on business." Apologetic at first, these unwelcome visitors grew threatening as their accounts went unpaid. Mr. Alcott frankly admitted the claims against him were just, but he was penniless. The truth was that Mr. Alcott, talented in so many ways, had no understanding of money — neither how to make it nor how to use it. By the end of 1839 he was $5,000 in debt.

Mrs. Alcott's father and brother helped. Her cousins, the Sewalls, brought dresses to be made over for the girls. Friends were kind. Just after the New Year, Mr. Emerson arrived and persuaded Mr. Alcott to visit him in Concord.

He stayed a week, enjoying walks in the beautiful countryside. He read in his host's well-stocked library. They had hours of rich talk together. They made plans that offered new hope for a better future.

Mr. Alcott came home full of excitement. He described the beauty he had seen — the wooded hills, the seven ponds set like jewels in the rolling fields, the rich soil, the meadows watered by two placid rivers — then he told his great news. They were going to leave Boston and go to live in Concord — a place whose very name meant peace and happiness.

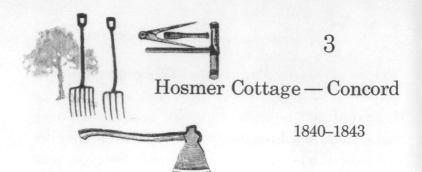

3

Hosmer Cottage — Concord

ON A WET DAY in April, the Alcotts came to their new home in Concord — Hosmer Cottage. Although it was small, so too was the rent of scarcely five dollars a month, and there was a barn, space for a vegetable garden, a tree-shaded yard, and a view across the mist-hung meadows to the slow, broad river. The promise of spring was everywhere — in the budding maples, the noisy frogs, the rushing brooks, the drifting fragrance of the arbutus.

"I'm glad we came," Louisa said. "This is better than Boston, isn't it, Father?"

Mr. Alcott, as always full of high hopes, agreed. "But our life here," he explained to the girls, "will be very different than it was in the city. There I was a teacher. Now I must earn our living by manual labor."

"What does that mean?" Anna asked.

"Using my hands as well as my head. Working as a woodcutter, a farm laborer, a carpenter."

"We'll help," Louisa and Anna said in one voice.

"We must give up many things," Mr. Alcott said. "More than ever before. We must raise our own food and buy as little as possible."

True to their word, the girls did help. Anna usually stayed indoors, dusting, drying dishes, and making the beds, but Louisa preferred to be outdoors with her father. Together they planted radishes, onions, peas, lettuce, and cabbage in neat, marked rows, and later, as the soil warmed, beans, melons, squash and corn. Louisa had a hen and hunted the eggs every day.

Friends and relatives came from Boston — their Sewall cousins, the Mays, Dr. Windship, his daughter who also was named Louisa, and his son Hamilton. Neighbors called — Mrs. Emerson, her arms full of flowers from her beautiful garden, Mr. Hosmer, their landlord, and his family, Mrs. Thoreau and her son Henry.

Henry Thoreau, twenty-two and a Harvard graduate, taught school, and he shared Mr. Alcott's theory that children learn best in a happy atmosphere. The two men soon found they thought alike on many subjects. Both were staunch abolitionists. Both, too, thought it wrong to pay taxes to a government that permitted such an evil thing as slavery to exist. Henry came so often to Hosmer Cottage that Louisa and her sisters adopted him as a kind of older brother. He loved the outdoors, as did all the Alcotts, and in their long walks together through the countryside, Thoreau showed the girls the wonders in fields and ponds that he would later describe in his great books.

In June, Louisa went back to Boston to spend a few

weeks with her mother's cousins, the Sewalls. Messages came from Hosmer Cottage every few days to tell her the news — the radishes were ripe, her hen had six little chicks, and ". . . the House Playroom, Dolls, Hoop, Garden, Flowers, Fields, Woods, Brooks," her father wrote, ". . . all miss the noisy little girl who used to make house and garden, barn and field, ring with her footsteps . . ."

At the end of July, the Sewalls told her the best news of all. She had a baby sister, Abby May Alcott.

"Please say to our Pet," said her father's letter, "that her new sister is fair and will look at her with joy, as will all others in the little cottage which she left six long weeks ago."

Louisa went home in early August. Mrs. Alcott, busy with little Abby, needed helping hands. Louisa did her best. She never enjoyed housework, nor did she do it as well as Anna, but now she learned to sweep and iron and dust with speed and skill. Once her chores were done she flew off to the fields to join her friends.

When the Alcotts had first moved to Concord, the village children thought "the stylish Boston girls" at Hosmer Cottage would never stir "out of the parlor." They soon discovered their mistake.

"No boy can be my friend till I beat him in a race," Louy Alcott immediately announced, ". . . and no girl can be my friend unless she climbs trees and leaps fences."

Young Cyrus Hosmer, their landlord's son, doubted that any girl could be quite as brave as their newcomer seemed. He decided to test her courage. He gave Louisa a dark brittle pod. "Dare you to rub this in your eye."

She obliged. She had never seen a dried red pepper before. Although her tears flowed the rest of the day, she refused to cry.

Cyrus was impressed, but not fully convinced. He jumped off the highest beam in the barn. Louisa, undaunted, followed his lead. She sprained both ankles. Someone found a wide board and carried her home on it. She endured the pain and kept quiet.

When she could walk again Cyrus coaxed her to chew tobacco. Her friends carried her home again, this time green and glassy-eyed, but still uncomplaining, in a wheelbarrow.

Then Cyrus admitted she had as much courage as any girl — or boy — he knew. Louisa held no grudge, and the two became fast friends.

When the Alcott's first summer in Concord drew to a close, Louisa helped her father gather in their small harvest against the winter. She and Anna and even little Beth collected chestnuts, walnuts, and butternuts. In the evening they sat around the fire and cut apples into neat slices for drying.

As they worked, Mr. Alcott told them stories of his boyhood on a rocky farm in Connecticut, how his mother taught him to read by marking the letters on the sanded hearth with a twig, how he made his own ink of oak and maple bark steeped in indigo, a plant used to dye homespun cloth blue. He described his journeys, too, as a young man through the South, peddling needles, threads, buttons, and notions.

When Thanksgiving came the Alcotts, surprisingly, discovered a family who had even less to live on than they did. With some contriving Mrs. Alcott managed to fill a basket for them with corn, the best of their winter squash, some brightly polished apples, a loaf of whole wheat bread, and, for a treat, a packet of maple sugar.

She and the girls delivered their offering on Thanksgiving morning. At every house they passed as they walked home feasts were in the making. Savory whiffs of roasting turkey, sage dressing, boiled onions, the spices in the pumpkin pies, filled the air. The Alcotts, remembering the sad-eyed, hungry children they had left, felt no envy and ate their own usual fare with extra thanks and rejoiced in an apple pudding for dessert.

December brought bitter, bone-cold weather. Anna and Louisa went to bed early to keep warm, huddling under the covers with their dolls and their books. Water froze in their pitcher. Mr. Alcott had to melt ice in the morning so they might wash their faces.

He usually rose first and made the family's bread, and quite often prepared breakfast for Anna and Louisa, as well. His ideas about food were unusual, and he once deeply offended a friend by mashing a potato into a dish of strawberries and eating the mixture. The girls, however, liked what he cooked for them, and they cherished the time they had alone with him in the warm kitchen before Mrs. Alcott, Beth, and the baby appeared. He answered all their questions seriously; he talked and read to them.

Mr. Alcott still taught the girls at home, and their studies occupied the greater part of each day. They worked sums, read, sketched, and wrote in their diaries. After their lessons were over, time often dragged. The chilling weather kept their friends indoors. Anna and Louisa wandered alone through the deserted garden, peeked into the empty barn where the wind whined, stood under the leafless trees.

"Let's go downtown," Louisa proposed one such bleak afternoon.

"We'd better ask Marmee," Anna said. Baby Abby's name for their mother had been adopted by all the girls.

Mrs. Alcott thought it too cold, but she let them go. She thought they could keep warmer walking than sitting by the little fire.

Concord was the scene of the first battle in the American Revolution. Sometimes Anna and Louisa followed the very same route that the Minute Men had taken on that fateful April day in 1776 when they gathered at the bridge to defy the redcoats and defend their rights as free men against the tyranny of the English king.

The old road was still a busy place. The girls saw drovers bringing cattle through to Boston from Vermont and New Hampshire. Teams of oxen, snorting steam in the frosty air, hauled wood. Concord was smaller and quieter than Boston, but Louisa could usually find something to interest her — men drilling on Muster Day, a politician making a speech, or a tinker mending a pot. Once they watched a clown with a trained horse that could pick up a cap from the ground and select cards from a pack. Often a friend beckoned Anna and Louisa into a warm kitchen to eat a fresh doughnut or carry a message to their mother.

This overcast day the roads were empty. House doors stayed shut, window curtains drawn against the cold. Anna and Louisa trudged home, tired, cold, and bored. Indoors they quarreled.

"You pinched me."

"I didn't!"

"You did!"

Mr. Alcott, hearing their bitter tones, left his books and called the girls to him. He took the two pairs of small hands in his and held them together. "Until Louisa and Anna can be gentle and kind to each other,"

he said, "they cannot have the pleasure of tending the baby."

Anna burst into tears. "I'd rather have almost any punishment than that."

Louisa, too, was contrite, and she resolved to do better. Only it seemed harder for her than for Anna. Her parents understood this and they tried earnestly to help her. It seemed to do little good to talk to her. In any case, the Alcotts did not believe that children should be scolded in public. How could their faults, particularly Louisa's, be corrected? Mrs. Alcott had an idea. She hung what she called a "budget basket" in the entry-way. Into it, she told the girls, she and their father would put little private notes for them.

"It will," she explained, "give us a daily opportunity to exchange thought and sentiment — and be a pleasant way of healing all differences . . ."

No one looked at the contents of the budget basket until supper was over. Then the girls took turns at playing postmaster, and delivered the messages in the basket to the addressees. These letters and the comments Mrs. Alcott wrote in her daughters' diaries were not always reproofs or criticisms. Words of love and praise were there, too. Mr. Alcott often made a little verse or drew pictures to point a moral.

For Louisa he once sketched two little children, one playing a harp, the other shooting an arrow, and beneath them:

> Two passions strong divide our life —
> Meek, gentle love, or boisterous strife. ،

"Meek and gentle" described Anna and Little Beth, and even Baby Abby May, Louisa had to admit. *She* was the boisterous one, with more energy than she knew how to use. She would try, she promised herself and her parents, to be more like her sisters.

Heavy snows fell. Perhaps that helped Louisa keep her resolution to be good. Her temper always improved when she could be outside, shoveling, sliding, building forts, setting up snowmen with charcoal eyes, watching her chance to aim a snowball at Cyrus Hosmer's head and getting two in return.

Cyrus Hosmer took Louisa coasting. All the Concord children had sleds of bright colors — green, yellow, blue — with bold names painted on the sides: Thunder Bolt, Dasher, Raceaway. They flashed down the hillsides and across the ice-covered ponds, shouting the traditional warning (no one knew just what it meant): "Clear the lulla! Clear the lulla!"

More than one rider came to grief in an upset or a collision, but Louisa, though daring as ever, had grown wiser, and she managed, despite a few spills, to walk home on her own two feet.

Christmas came. Their cousin Hamilton Windship made two trips over from Boston, his arms full of presents each time — shoes, warm flannel cloth to make into dresses, a silk work bag, and, best of all, books. Louisa found the bright gilt of the bindings, the uncut pages irresistible. They read them all — *Northcote's Fables, Scripture History, Mother Goose's Melody,* and *The Alphabet of Natural History.* What a feast!

After the holidays Mr. Alcott's chances for work grew less and less. Plowing, planting, mowing, and husking were long over for the year. The corn was all shelled. No one seemed to need a carpenter. He could count on little but a day of wood chopping now and then, or perhaps, on rare occasions, an invitation to give one of his conversation-lectures in a neighboring town. Mrs. Alcott took in sewing — her needle flashing in and out — to add a dollar to their slim purse. When the girls helped she paid them for their share.

The Alcotts might have managed except for a constant stream of visitors. It sometimes seemed as if every reformer in the country, every hoper, dreamer, and seeker, found his way to the Alcotts' door. Coming home from a walk, Louisa and Anna never knew whom they would find sitting beside their fire, perhaps eating their last piece of bread.

One day it was a pair of bearded men, barefoot and in ragged clothes, who stayed until Sunday and then stood outside the church door and shouted all through the service for the congregation to "Come out! Come out! Worship God without ministers."

After the Come-outers went on their way, a phrenologist arrived. He pinned charts of the human cranium on the Alcotts' wall, and Louisa and Anna watched him measure Mr. Alcott's long, narrow head and then "analyze" his character from the "bumps" on his skull.

Next, a follower of the preacher William Miller stopped to warn the Alcotts that almost immediately the world was going to end. With him was a "doctor" who was sure he could cure all the diseases of mankind with water.

Mrs. Alcott sometimes lost patience with these visitors, but Mr. Alcott listened carefully to what they had to say. He realized it was a time of change in America. The institutions and ideals that had served the young republic of 1776 were inadequate for an expanding nation now fifty-years-old. Many men sought an answer to the increasingly complex problems of life; many were positive they had found the perfect solution and set out to convince others. If some of these reformers wasted their efforts on impossible cures for imaginary ills, others corrected grave social injustices and helped make that better world they all sought.

Louisa and her sisters, sitting in the little kitchen at Hosmer Cottage, heard proposed scores of ways to help mankind — eat whole grains, let the women vote and wear trousers, find a universal language, close the saloons, forget money, prohibit child labor, live in an octagon house, free the slaves, make education compulsory, join one of a dozen new religions. Any sincere believer could be sure of a cordial reception at the Alcotts', whether or not his host fully agreed with his doctrines.

As their visitors increased, the Alcotts' supplies grew less and less. Their flour barrel was empty. The cool cellar held only a few apples and squash and some potatoes. Mr. Alcott had to ask for credit at the store. Spring and planting time seemed a long way off.

Yet perhaps not. Louisa found a starved and almost frozen bird in the garden. She warmed and fed it, stroking the head and the rusty red breast. After the bird, strong again, had flown away, Louisa sat for a long time at her desk, writing on her slate, erasing, writing again, crossing out lines, rewriting.

That night, after supper was over, the dishes washed,

and everyone settled down around the table, Louisa said, "Would you like me to read a poem?"

Her father laid aside his book, courteously attentive as always to his children's words.

Mrs. Alcott looked up from her sewing. "What is the title?"

"To the First Robin."

Anna and little Beth drew close to listen as Louisa began:

> Welcome, welcome, little stranger,
> Fear no harm, and fear no danger;
> We are glad to see you here,
> For you sing "Sweet Spring is near."
>
> Now the white snow melts away;
> Now the flowers blossom gay;
> Come, dear bird, and build your nest,
> For we love our robin best.

"I am not familiar with this poem," Mr. Alcott said. "Who wrote it?"

"I did, Father," Louisa said.

"*You* did?"

"Yes, sir."

"All by yourself, Louy?" Anna's voice was full of pride.

"All by myself."

The whole family smiled in agreement when Marmee fondly declared, "You will grow up a Shakespeare!"

So Louisa, although only eight years old, began her career. From then on she wrote — more poems, stories, plays, entries in her journal. Even more important, she was storing up memories of people and places, of characters, incidents, and scenes that would, in years to come, fill thirty volumes and make Louisa May Alcott a beloved name to readers all over the world.

4

Fruitlands

1843

AFTER THREE YEARS in Concord, the Alcotts were deeper in debt than ever. Mrs. Alcott's brother, Samuel May, and many other friends and relatives helped with gifts of money, clothes, and food. Often after Mr. Emerson had paid a visit to Hosmer Cottage a crisp bank note would be found under the clock, or a gold piece tumbled out of a teacup.

It required more than this to support a family of six and the unending stream of visitors. The Alcotts' situation was desperate when, in the spring of 1843, an important letter came from England. A group of men who had read and liked Mr. Alcott's book on education wanted him to visit their country and see the school they had started and named in his honor, Alcott House.

Sitting in the kitchen of the little cottage the whole family discussed the invitation. At first Mr. Alcott declared it was impossible for him to leave home. Mrs. Alcott, knowing how much the trip meant to him, urged him to go. With her usual courage she assured him she could "manage" while he was away. The girls, too, promised to help.

"But who will plow the garden, chop wood, keep

the fires going, carry the water?" Mr. Alcott asked.

"I will," Louisa said.

Mr. Alcott shook his head doubtfully. Even if Louisa could do all those chores, he had no money for his ticket, traveling expenses, and clothes. Sadly he decided that he must forget the whole idea.

When Mr. Emerson learned of the invitation, he generously offered to pay for the journey. On May 7, 1842, Mr. Alcott sailed for England aboard the *Rosalind,* a round-trip ticket and a hundred dollars in gold in his shabby, red pocketbook. His brother Junius came from Connecticut to be the man of the house until his return.

The girls missed their father, but their uncle, only ten years older than Anna, did his best to amuse them. He took them out in his boat *The Undine.* They dabbled in the marshes along the river's edge, pretending they were Indians hunting flag roots, squaws braiding rushes, mermaids singing to sailors, and Robinson Crusoe on his island.

Plays like these still entertained Beth, who was only seven, but Anna, now eleven, and Louisa, ten, wanted more challenging roles. With the help of their friends they started a theater in the barn at Hosmer Cottage. Old sheets pinned on a clothesline served for a curtain. Scenery was simple — a few pine branches became a forest, sacking thrown over a sawhorse a cave.

"But we need costumes," Louisa told her mother.

Mrs. Alcott gave the girls a trunk of old finery that had once belonged to her aunt, the famous Dolly Q., the greatest beauty of her time. As the wife of John Hancock, first signer of the Declaration of Independence and Governor of Massachusetts, Aunt Dolly Q. had entertained George Washington, Lafayette, Paul Revere, Samuel Adams — all the great and famous of the age.

Louisa and her sister never saw this legendary figure, who died before their birth, but they knew all about her. Imperious and stubborn, she once made Mr. Alcott eat four slices of beef at her dinner table. She had lost her great fortune, but she kept her style and charm and fine figure to the end of her life.

Louisa and her sisters asked no better legacy from

their Aunt Dolly Quincy Hancock Scott than her trunk, which now became their costume box. Her tiny satin shoes, tattered brocades, broken fans, split gloves dressed them for any part — a long cloak, a dashing hat, a piece of plume made a cavalier; a red scarf, a paper knife dagger, and a false moustache, a pirate. Louisa learned to create superb effects from very little.

The girls wrote to their father and told him the news of their theater. When they did "Jack and the Beanstalk," the Giant accidentally fell out of his "sky" in the hayloft and everybody laughed. The coach they made for the performance of "Cinderella" looked like a real pumpkin. Next they were going to do the "Snow Maiden," and after that "Little Henry and the Gypsies."

Mr. Alcott answered their letters, saying he thought of them all. He missed his Louisa, ". . . with her quick and ready senses, her agile limbs, and boundless curiosity, her penetrating mind and tear-shedding heart alive to all moving, breathing things . . ."

His letter added that, when he returned, some friends would be with him. Great plans were in the making. They were going to live a new life in a new place. They would leave Concord and the materialistic world where men toiled for money, and, with others like themselves, form a colony devoted to peace and beauty.

On a bright October day, Mr. Alcott came home, accompanied by a Mr. Lane and his son William, who joined the household.

A boy *might* be an addition, the girls decided. William was about ten, a quiet, solemn child with brown eyes and brown hair.

"He has a kind of a William Penn face," Louisa whispered to her sisters.

They could not always understand William. He sounded his words oddly; he called cookies biscuits; he had never eaten corn or squash or their favorite dessert, apple slump.

"Apple slump! What's that?" William asked.

"Everybody knows what apple slump is," Anna said.

"I don't," William insisted.

"It's sliced apples in a deep dish," Louisa explained, "with a top of biscuit dough."

"Rich biscuit dough," Anna said, "baked crusty brown and served upside down — "

"With molasses sauce," Beth added. "Lots of molasses sauce poured over it."

William thought he would like to try apple slump. Except for the alarming habit of falling fast asleep in the middle of a game or a conversation, he was an agreeable companion.

The children had ample time to make friends during the weeks that followed. Mr. Lane and Mr. Alcott were away searching for the perfect site for their new home. Finally, Mr. Lane bought one hundred acres near the village of Still River, about fifteen miles from Concord. Mr. Alcott doubted the fertility of the soil, but he agreed to the selection.

Sitting around the table at Hosmer Cottage, the two families made wonderful plans. Mr. Alcott's hair was graying and his face was lined, but his blue eyes were radiant, and his voice young, as he described his dream of the future. The new colony, which they decided to call Fruitlands, was to be a refuge, a haven of peace. There, away from the evils of the world, from slavery, war, greed, the struggle for money and possessions, men of goodwill would come to live and work and build another Eden.

Louisa, listening, caught her father's enthusiasm, his joy. This idea of a new life in a new place appealed to her adventurous spirit and her idealistic nature. Her spirits soared as the days flew by. She worked hard indoors and out, collecting, sorting, and packing their possessions. Too busy to quarrel with Anna, to tease Beth, to fall into mischief, she stopped only long enough to exclaim, "Mother, why am I so happy?"

Finally everything was ready. Louisa never forgot that stormy day in June when they set out for their promised land. Long afterward, in a story, she described their journey. Atop a wagon piled high with their household goods sat Mrs. Alcott, beneath a big umbrella; she held Abby in her lap. On one side were Anna and Beth, wrapped in a big shawl, clutching their dolls; on the other was William Lane, balancing the bust of Socrates on his knees. Mr. Alcott, in a long blue cloak, walked ahead. Splashing along beside him, indifferent to rain, hail, wind, and mud puddles, was eleven-year-old Louisa.

Over rolling hills, through oak forests, across rushing brooks, they plodded until, late in the afternoon, they came to the top of a high ridge. Here they turned and followed a cart track that led them just at dusk to a red house on a hillside.

The news of their venture had already brought recruits to the colony. Joseph Palmer, an elderly gentleman in a white robe, came out to greet them. He re-

minded Louisa of a bride, despite his long beard.

Abraham Everett, a dark, melancholy man wearing a rough, homespun suit, joined them around the big fireplace for a supper of roasted potatoes and brown bread.

Tired after the long journey, the girls soon went to bed and fell fast asleep. When they awoke in the morning, it was to a scene of dazzling beauty. Below them spread a broad valley bathed in sun, bordered far to the westward by a chain of hills, and beyond those, fifty miles away in New Hampshire, towered the peaks on Monadnock and Ascutney. There was much to see close to home too. After breakfast the girls set out to explore the house, the garden, the rising fields to the east, the woods, and the brook.

Fruitlands, it soon became apparent, was an overly optimistic choice of name. The orchard consisted of only ten gnarled, old apple trees. The house, cheerless and in need of repair, reminded Mrs. Alcott of "a refined pigsty." With her usual courage, however, she set to work to create a home with the materials at hand.

The entry hall, she decided, was wide enough to house the library. Mr. Alcott built shelves for the thousand rare books he and Mr. Lane had brought from England. A room to the left of the hall would be a study, one to the right a refectory, and beyond these, extending the full width of the house, was the common room or kitchen. Upstairs there were several small bedrooms, and, above those, a low-roofed garret where the girls slept.

In the days that followed their arrival at Fruitlands, plans were made and rules established that would insure a perfect existence — or so everyone believed.

"We all agree," Mr. Lane said, "that nothing is to be admitted to the colony which has caused wrong or death to man or beast."

"This means," Mr. Alcott explained to the girls, "that we shall not use rice, cotton, molasses, or spices produced by slave labor. We must also do without meat, eggs, milk, cheese, butter, or wool, for all these are stolen from animals."

"Neither shall lamps be permitted," Mr. Lane added severely, "for they burn whale oil."

It was also decided that salt, as well as stimulants such as tea, coffee, and chocolate were unwholesome and those items, too, should be banned.

"What *will* we eat, Father?" Louisa asked.

"Whole grains, maple syrup, nuts, fruits, and vegetables," Mr. Alcott said.

"If we can't wear wool or cotton, what will our dresses be made from, Father?"

"I have planted a field of flax for linen and set out two mulberry trees to feed silk worms."

Mrs. Alcott sighed. She knew that long before a yard of material could come from these sources, the girls would have outgrown all their clothing.

The Fruitland colonists also believed it would be wrong to plow or fertilize the land, since that required animals.

"The spade will be our only tool," Mr. Alcott declared.

One day of digging in the heavy soil, however, proved this idea impractical. As a compromise, an ox and a cow were yoked together (to the astonishment of the neighboring farmers), and with this team the ground was prepared for planting the crops.

The Fruitlands colony was not the only experiment of its kind. Many others, founded in the same way, existed in nineteenth-century America. The Alcotts were soon invited to visit a religious group called "Shakers," who had also "left the world" in order to lead more perfect lives. These devout people stayed in their own peaceful, secluded community a few miles away. Their big barns were full of grain; sleek cattle grazed in the meadows. They had a dairy, a knitting room, a wood shop, an ice house, well-stocked pantries, and cool cellars. Everything was clean, beautiful, and orderly.

The Shakers raised herbs and sold nearly ten thousand pounds of them every year. Louisa and Anna walked through the neat gardens and watched the women gathering lavender, damask roses, savory, sage, and lemon balm in flat baskets for drying. The golden humming of the bees filled the fragrant air. Everyone was happy; everyone was busy. The Shakers followed one law, the Golden Rule, and they prospered.

The Fruitlands family took heart. Surely they, too, might do the same, if they worked hard. They rose at dawn, bathed in icy water, and then donned tunics and loose trousers of white linen. Thus attired, they sat down to their morning meal of fruit or berries and whole wheat bread baked in fanciful images of animals or flowers.

Mr. Lane made out a schedule that filled their days with lessons for the children and tasks indoors and out for all. Slowly the fields were cleared, grain was sowed, and vegetables were planted. In late June everyone helped mow the hay. It was a momentous occasion. They carried this first fruit of their labors ceremoniously to the barn, with uncovered heads, rejoicing as they went.

Some hours were found for merrymaking. After supper they usually had music and dancing in the common room. As a special celebration in honor of Beth's birthday, the household rose at five and marched up the hill, singing, to a pine tree hung with presents. On a mossy throne Beth, crowned with leaves, accepted their homage. Mr. Lane played his violin. Mr. Alcott read a parable. Each of the others offered her a flower emblematic of their wish for her. Anna's was a rose for purity and love; Louisa's a lily of the valley for innocence.

"And here's mine," little Abby said. "Wake robins. But I don't know what they mean."

Beth had other gifts — a silk-thread balloon from her mother, a fan from Anna, a little pitcher from Abby, a pincushion from Louisa. Even William woke up long enough to present her with a book. As they trooped home through the daisy-strewn fields, squirrels chattered overhead, rabbits leaped in the hedge rows, and thrushes answered Mr. Lane's fiddle tunes.

The children, when lessons and chores were done, found plenty of amusement outdoors. Louisa described some of their games in her diary:

> I ran in the wind and played to be a horse and had a lovely time in the woods with Anna and Lizzie. We were fairies, and made gowns and paper wings, I "flied" highest of all.

They took long walks, too, with their parents, discovering treasures along the way — a deer's cast horn, a jay's feather turning blue, a wild grapevine curled into a swing. As they strolled or rested in the shade of the great trees, Mr. Alcott recited poetry and told them stories, listened to their chatter, and answered all their questions.

The fame of the Fruitlands colony spread. Weekly their numbers grew, and some of the new arrivals were very odd indeed. One man slept by day. At night Louisa and Anna heard him crowing as he wandered through the fields. Another visitor announced he had lived a whole year on nothing but soda crackers — now he intended to try a year on apples. Many more, equally eccentric, came, tarried a little while, and then went on their way, still seeking.

Mrs. Alcott's burdens increased. Visitors meant more work for her — more cooking, more washing, more ironing. Silent Abraham Everett helped her as best he could. The girls swept, made the beds, dusted, and ran errands, but Louisa, watching her tired mother, longed to do more. She wrote a poem:

To Mother

I hope that soon, dear Mother,
   You and I may be
In the quiet room my fancy
   Has so often made for thee —

The pleasant, sunny chamber,
   The cushioned easy chair,
The book laid for your reading,
   The vase of flowers fair;

The desk beside the window
   Where the sun shines warm and bright
And there is ease and quiet
   The promised book you write;

While I sit close beside you,
   Content at last to see
That you can rest, dear mother,
   And I can cherish thee.

One day, she promised herself, she would make it come true.

Friends from Boston and Concord, who rode over to see how the Alcotts fared, departed full of doubts. Somehow things were not going well at Fruitlands. The garden produced few vegetables. The girls and William, when he could be roused to action, gathered purslane, a wild green, and Mrs. Alcott cooked that. A little corn ripened, but it was soon eaten. By accident, at planting time three kinds of grain had been sown in the largest field. Only a small stand of barley resulted.

"Every bit of it must be saved," Mrs. Alcott said, "if we are to have any bread for the winter."

Then men cut the precious crop and bound it into sheaves, stacking them to dry in the field. Then they went off on a lecture tour to spread their new gospel.

The day after their departure, Mrs. Alcott noticed dark clouds in the eastern sky, a sure sign of rain. She

quickly gathered all her sheets in a clothes basket and, calling the children to follow her, ran to the barley field.

"Collect sheaves," she said, "and stack them on a sheet. Then if we each take a corner we can carry a good-sized load to the barn."

William followed Mrs. Alcott's directions as obediently as the girls, but he was puzzled, and he whispered to Louisa, "Why are we doing this?"

She gave him a scornful glance. "So the grain won't be rained on."

"But isn't rain good for grain?"

"Only while it's growing," Louisa explained. "If cut grain gets wet, it molds. Then we can't eat it. *Everybody* who lives in the country knows *that!*"

All afternoon they worked, carrying load after load. The heat rose in shimmering waves from the valley. Back and forth they ran with more sheaves, and more, and still more. They dared not rest, or even take time to go to the brook for a drink of cold water. Another load was in, and another. More than half the field was done. Thunder rumbled beyond the mountains. Hurry! Another load. Another. Could they finish? As the horizon darkened and lightning flashed, they raced against the storm and won. When at last the rain came in a swirling fury, it fell upon an empty field. The barley was safe and dry inside the barn.

Mrs. Alcott, understandably, felt the men should

have been there to help. When they returned from their jaunt, her quick temper flared. Harvesting their crops for the winter stores was more important, she told them, than gaining new recruits.

Mr. Lane answered sharply; criticism, particularly from a woman, he could neither accept nor forgive. In the days that followed, he showed his resentment in petty ways. He scolded the girls during their lesson period. Anna looked hurt. Beth wept. Louisa stamped out of the room. Even in their leisure hours Mr. Lane's critical eye seemed always upon them. He saw Louisa petting a kitten. The next day in class he ordered the girls to make a list of their faults.

"And, Louisa," he said, "be sure to put down your love of cats."

Any show of affection roused his ire. Baby Abby was quite spoiled, he pointed out, because Louisa and Anna held her and played with her so much.

October the eighth was Mrs. Alcott's birthday, but the day was not a happy one. Louisa wrote in her journal that night:

> October 8th — When I woke up, the first thought I got was "It's Mother's birthday; I must be very good." I ran and wished her a happy birthday, and gave her my kiss. After breakfast we gave her our presents. I had a moss cross and a piece of poetry for her.

We did not have any school and played in the woods and got red leaves. In the evening we danced and sang and I read a story about "Contentment." I wish I was rich, I was good, and we were all a happy family this day.

More and more of the rules made when the colony began were proving impractical, if not impossible, to follow. The flickering flame of the bayberry candles, for example, did not give Mrs. Alcott enough light for her sewing. She found a whale-oil lamp and defiantly set it on the table. The company quickly forgot their concern for whales and drew close to the better light with their books.

The first snow came, covering the fields and blotting out the valley, and the children shivered in their linen tunics. No amount of running could make them warm. Louisa developed a cough and a sharp pain in her side. William, too, fell ill. Mrs. Alcott nursed both children with the same tender care, although far from well herself. Because her teeth were poor, she was unable to chew the nuts, hard apples, and coarse bread, now their only food, and she was slowly starving.

The children soon sensed that something was wrong, although at first they scarcely knew what. Day by day the community grew smaller, and Mr. Lane more dissatisfied, cold, and distant. Several times he reminded Mrs. Alcott that it was *his* money that had paid some of their Concord debts and bought Fruitlands. Meals were silent affairs. No one felt like singing or dancing in the evenings now as they had at first. Mr. Lane glowered in the corner, his violin forgotten.

Gradually the older children realized that a bitter struggle was raging in the little community where peace was to have reigned. It was clear to Mrs. Alcott that they could not exist through the winter at Fruitlands. They must abandon the experiment or starve. She had her girls to consider. Her concern for her family irked Mr. Lane. He seemed to think a wife and children were burdens to any man, and that Mr. Alcott, in particular, would be a much greater philosopher if he lived apart from Mrs. Alcott and the girls. Mr. Alcott, torn between his dream and his family, seemed bewildered.

Anna went to Boston to visit some relatives. Beth and Abby were too young to understand. Louisa suffered alone. Long after she went to bed, she could hear the voices below, pleading, demanding, accusing. She had no one to share her anxiety and her fear, no one to talk to. What was happening? Why were they quarreling downstairs? Why did her mother cry? Was her mother going away? Would her father come, too? If not, what would they do without him? Where would they live? Would she be sent to stay with relatives, alone, with no parents, no sisters, no home? She was afraid to ask the questions. She was afraid to hear the answers.

When Anna returned from Boston after Thanksgiving, Mr. and Mrs. Alcott explained to the girls that some changes were in prospect, although nothing definite had been decided. Louisa feared the worst. Her heart was heavy that night when she wrote in her diary:

> I did my lessons and walked in the afternoon. Father read to us in dear Pilgrim's Progress. Mr. L. was in Boston and we were glad. In the eve father and mother and I had a long talk. I was very unhappy and we all cried. Anna and I cried in bed and I prayed God to keep us all together.

Louisa's prayer was answered. Four weeks later Mr. Lane walked into the house one day, went upstairs, came down with his clothes packed in a case.

"Come," he said to William, who was sitting at the table with the girls, "we are leaving here for good."

Startled, William rose and struggled into his coat.

"Go outside," Mr. Lane ordered him. "At once!"

The boy obeyed.

"Mayn't we even bid him goodbye, sir?" Louisa asked.

"No," Mr. Lane said curtly. He turned to Mrs. Al-

cott, sitting silently by. "Before I go, let me remind you that *I* am the legal owner of this property. You may not burn *my* wood. You may not grind *my* corn for your own use."

The door closed behind him. To Mr. Alcott it was a crushing loss. He did not care that the wood, the corn, even the farm itself, were no longer his. To him material things meant little. He lived by hope and faith — hope for a world of peace and beauty, faith that men of goodwill working together could achieve it. Consequently, when the Fruitlands experiment failed, he had nothing to sustain him. He lay mute, his face to the wall, refusing food, water, even words of comfort.

Mrs. Alcott rose to the emergency. She treated her husband with home remedies, spearmint tea and a stew of dried blackberries. She sold her best cloak for twelve dollars and a treasured silver slicer for twenty dollars. Ten more dollars came from her brother Samuel. She sent word to Still River, the village five miles away, and rented four rooms in the Lovejoy farmhouse, and engaged a sled to move her family and their few possessions there.

Early in the new year of 1844, the Alcotts left Fruitlands forever — poor, sad, and weary — but together.

5

Still River and Concord

1844–1848

SLOWLY Mr. Alcott's health and spirits improved. Away from the troubled atmosphere of Fruitlands, with companions of their own age, the girls bloomed. Louisa wrote in her diary:

> Life is pleasanter than it used to be, and I don't care about dying any more. Had a splendid run . . . Sat and heard the pines sing a long time. I had a pleasant time with my mind, for it was happy.

Warm woolen clothing and other necessities came from the relatives in Boston. The Lovejoys proved kind and generous to their tenants and the children of the two families were inseparable.

A more varied diet was possible than Mr. Lane's strict supervision had allowed. They still omitted meat, but now Mrs. Alcott could enjoy the luxury of a cup of tea. The girls went to church suppers and picnics. Although shocked at first by the lavishness of the spreads, they learned to eat many new foods.

The neighbors, forgetting all the stories about the

cranks at Fruitlands, soon succumbed to the Alcott charm. The girls attended the summer session of the village school — their first experience in an ordinary classroom, and enjoyed it thoroughly.

On Beth's tenth birthday, Anna and Louisa invited some of their new friends to an entertainment in her honor. Mrs. Lovejoy's parlor served as a stage, and the audience sat in the dining room. First Anna, dressed in kilts, gave a Scotch ballad. Then Louisa, the star, appeared. In a robe trimmed with feathers, her face, neck, arms, and ankles stained with walnut juice, she declaimed *Wild Roved an Indian Girl, Bright Alfarata.* Later, brandishing a shield, and sword, she recited a blood-curdling passage from "Ossian," and finally, as an encore, a dramatic poem, "Geehale's Lament." After the applause had died down, the whole company feasted on birthday cake and bowls of luscious cherries.

A few days after the party, Mrs. Alcott went to Boston to see her brother. Returning in the stage coach with her was another passenger, a lively, handsome boy of fourteen. She soon made friends with him.

His name was Frederick Llewellyn Hovey Willis. ". . . but call me Llewellyn . . ." he said. His father and mother were dead. He lived in Cambridge with his grandparents. "They're very strict." He was expelled from church before he was twelve as a heretic,

". . . Because I didn't believe in foreordination . . ." He loved the theater, ". . . Sometimes I slip out and go to a play in Boston." He was on his way to Still River to spend his vacation as a boarder on a farm.

At one of the stops the driver accidentally slammed the coach door on the boy's hand. He fainted.

Mrs. Alcott revived him. When Llewellyn opened his eyes, he saw what he always called "the dearest, kindest, most motherly face I ever beheld looking into mine."

She dressed his crushed fingers. Then, during the rest of the journey, she tried her best to divert him by telling stories of her girls and their escapades.

The next day Llewellyn came to call on Mrs. Alcott, but he did not find her at home. Neither he nor the four girls who received him could think of anything to say. They sat looking at each other in tongue-tied silence as the minutes dragged by. Finally Louisa could endure it no longer. She jumped up. "Let's run in the garden."

Out she dashed, Llewellyn and her sisters after her in a wild chase. From that time on, they played and chattered like old friends.

After the Alcotts moved to larger quarters, Llewellyn, with his grandparents' consent, was installed as a paying guest for the rest of the summer — and soon he was sharing in all their joys and sorrows.

He and Louisa and Anna went off on all-day excursions, trundling their books, lunches, and wraps in a three-wheeled barrow. They waded in the ponds and played tag. Louisa climbed trees with him and came home with her clothes torn and muddy.

The Alcotts had always wanted a boy and they still mourned their only son who had died at birth. Llewellyn filled an important place in the household. He loved Mrs. Alcott dearly, and as long as he lived, he remembered her kindness to him and to others. Seventy years later he said of her:

. . . though poverty and frequent actual want
were ever at her door, she had always a word of
counsel, encouragement and cheer. She never
turned a deaf ear to any appeal . . . and frequently shared her own scanty store with others
. . . I can think of but one other woman . . . during my entire life who so fully represented sympathy, love and tenderness . . .

Marmee, in return, gave him her deep affection and
full confidence. "This dear boy," she told her friends,
"is my little comforter."

In the fall, Llewellyn went back to his school in
Cambridge. The Alcotts lingered on in Still River,
with no prospects for the future. Mrs. Alcott did sewing and, since her friends kept her well supplied with
work, earned a little. Mr. Alcott chopped wood, helped
a neighbor or a farmer for a day or a week, and
occasionally he was invited to give a Conversation and
received a small fee.

The failure of Fruitlands changed Mr. Alcott. He
became less of a reformer, more of a philosopher. He
kept his basic beliefs — a concern for spiritual rather
than material things, an abhorrence of cruelty to man
or beast, a faith in God's goodness. However, he no
longer tried to convert others to his way of thinking
as he once had. He did not immediately relinquish
his dream of life in a colony away from the world. He

visited the Shakers again. He and Mrs. Alcott went, also, to Brook Farm and the Oneida Community. In all of these places, groups of people who shared a common goal lived together harmoniously, pursuing what they believed to be the ideal existence. None of these establishments seemed to offer Mr. Alcott what he wanted. He came to the conclusion that he would be happiest with just his own family under his own roof.

Fortunately, it became possible for him to do this. Shortly before the move to Fruitlands, Mrs. Alcott's father, Colonel May, died and left her a small sum to be used for a home. Now the estate was settled and Mrs. Alcott bought with her legacy a thirty-acre farm in Concord on the Lexington Road, a short walk from the Emersons, a mile and a half from the center of the village.

Late in the fall, the Alcotts left Still River by stage, Louisa riding on top beside the driver as far as Littleton. There they boarded the New Fitchburg Railway — the first time the girls had ever ridden on "the cars." The bell rang, the whistles blew, the engine coughed sparks and cinders, and they started off.

Railroads were still a novelty and depots a favorite meeting place. A crowd usually turned out to see the daily train pull in — or race by at the unbelievable speed of twenty miles an hour. So, on an October day in 1844, all of Concord saw, or soon heard, that the

Alcotts, who went off in a wagon, had come back in grand style.

Their triumphant arrival was dimmed by their first view of their new home, a dilapidated farmhouse built almost a hundred and fifty years before, and remodeled many times. It stood, with a wheelwright's shop and a barn, in a morass of rubbish, the garden rooted into humps by the previous tenant's pigs.

Another Alcott folly! Louisa May, now twelve, and Anna, fourteen, were old enough to sense ridicule and, even worse, pity, when townspeople called. Their father went his serene way, caught in a new dream.

Connecticut men seemed to be born craftsmen — clockmakers, gunsmiths, tinkers, inventors — and Mr.

Alcott was no exception. The skills he learned in his boyhood now served him well With a helper he moved the barn to open the view across the meadow to the river. The shop, cut in two, made a wing at either end of the house. He threw two small rooms into a big kitchen, restored the well, and piped water into the house, a luxury in those days. He installed a bath with a shower bucket so light that even little Abby could raise it by a pulley and douse herself with the contents. He even contrived a clothes drier on a back porch by installing wooden rods next to the warm outer chimney wall. He terraced the hillside, transplanted trees and shrubs from the woods, improved the grounds, and built a summer house to adorn the hillside.

The girls worked, too. Louisa and Anna cleaned, painted, and papered. Beth and little Abby dug clumps of wild violets to border the garden. When they were finished, pretty chintz curtains hung at the windows, a cool matting covered the floor, vases of fresh flowers were everywhere. The old farmhouse became Hillside, a dignified mansion. Whatever Mr. Alcott's ability as an educator or a philosopher, Concord had to concede that few could equal him as a builder or gardener.

When Llewellyn Willis arrived to spend the summer with the Alcotts, he was introduced to all the delights of the new establishment — a huge attic, wide porches, winding staircases, any number of passageways, corners, crannies, and cupboards, and, best of all, a secret closet next to the chimney. The days overflowed with living.

The girls still studied with their father, and for a few months Anna and Louisa attended the district school. Later, little Ellen Emerson, who was about Beth's age, and her younger sister Edith shared their governess with the Alcotts. In her journal Louisa described their classes:

> Thursday . . . Miss Ford gave us a botany lesson in the woods. I am always good there. In the evening Miss Ford told us about the bones in our bodies and how they get out of order. I must be careful of mine, I climb and jump and run so much.

For Louisa was still a tomboy, leaping gates and dashing across the fields. ". . . The prettiest girl runner I ever saw," Llewellyn said. Her long chestnut hair streaming in the wind, she rolled her hoop from her own gate to the foot of Hardy's Hill, more than a mile, and, without stopping, turned and raced home again. No one then or since ever bettered her record.

All of the Alcotts loved the outdoors. Winter and summer they went for long walks. Often they stopped at Walden Pond where their friend Henry Thoreau now lived in a little hut built with his own hands. He sometimes gave them lunch — the thin bread he baked on hot stones, fresh corn, or perhaps wild berries.

Besides Henry Thoreau and Mr. Emerson, several other famous men now lived in Concord, among them Nathaniel Hawthorne, who wrote *Twice-Told Tales* and *Mosses from an Old Manse*, William Henry Channing, a brilliant and beloved Unitarian minister, and Ephraim Bull, a superb gardener who developed the Concord grape from a wild seedling.

The children of these families were friends of Louisa and her sisters and invitations flew between the houses. The girls' diaries record the good times they enjoyed — picnics on the cliffs, sailing on the river, parties to eat

the first cherries or plums of the season, May Day festivals where they all danced around the Maypole, fireworks on the Fourth of July.

Looking back, Louisa always called this time at Hillside the "happiest years." It is doubtful, however, that her father and mother would have completely agreed, for Louisa, always the most difficult of their children, was still a problem. Anna, at fifteen even-tempered and dependable, caused them no concern; Beth, nearly eleven, had a gentle goodness that won her the title of "Miss Tranquility"; Abby, although only five, already behaved like a little lady. Louisa, a willful child, had become, at thirteen, what her father called a "tempestuous" girl. Obstinate, disobedient, quarrelsome, by turns sulky and impudent, she was in one scrape after another. What new mischief her lively imagination would suggest no one could ever predict.

Walking with a younger girl, Clara Gowing, Louisa saw an unattended wagon at the curb.

"Let's take a ride, Clara."

"Oh, no, Louy." Clara shook her head. "We mustn't."

Louisa jumped up on the seat. "Come on, Clara. You're afraid."

Stung by the reproach, Clara climbed in. Louisa gave the horses a smart smack with the reins. "Get up."

Off they went through the quiet town, up one street

and down the next, dashing past other teams and sending startled pedestrians scurrying to safety.

"Please, please, Louisa, stop and let me out," Clara begged as they careened around a corner on two wheels. "Please!"

At last Louisa, tired of the game, halted the horses, and she and Clara climbed down to face the irate farmer who owned the wagon.

She was scolded and made to eat her supper alone. Punishment had little effect on her behavior. Cleaning house, she bruised her knee on a chair. The chair was guilty, she decided. She hung the culprit out the window on a string as compensation for her injuries. When her mother objected, Louisa answered disrespectfully and was shut in her room. In a fit of temper she soused her head with whale oil.

When her mother quietly helped her wash her long hair, Louisa felt remorseful.

"I'm sorry, Marmee. I'll do better."

She really tried, and sometimes she succeeded. Then Mrs. Alcott, who still read the girls' journals and often added her comments, wrote encouragingly to Louisa:

I have observed all day your patience with the baby, your obedience to me, your kindness to all. Go on "trying," my child; God will give you strength and courage and help you fill each day

with words and deeds of love. I shall lay this on
your pillow, put a warm kiss on your lips and say
a little prayer over you in your sleep. Mother.

For a few days, perhaps a week, all went well.
Louisa stopped teasing Abby. She and Beth helped
Mr. Alcott weed the garden and pick beans. Then
Louisa's temper flared. She quarreled with Anna.

"You're mean!" she cried. "Mean! *Mean!* MEAN!"

Mr. Alcott heard her angry voice and came out from
his study. "Look up that word in the dictionary,
Louisa May."

Mutinously she turned the pages — K . . . L . . .
M . . .

"What does it mean?" Mr. Alcott asked.

"Base and contemptible . . ." Louisa read the defi-
nition and burst into tears. "Father, I'm so ashamed I
called my dear sister that. Oh, my bad tongue and
temper . . ."

Her mother wrote in Louisa's journal:

My Louy, — I was grieved at your selfish behavior this morning, but also greatly pleased to
find you bore so meekly Father's reproof for it.
That is the way, dear; if you find you are wrong,
take the discipline sweetly, and do so no more
. . . I know that you will have a happy day after
the storm and gentle shower; keep quiet, read,

walk, but do not talk much till all is peace again.
Mother.

All *was* peace again — for a few days. Louisa did
her chores cheerfully. She spoke gently to Anna. She
took Abby walking. She offered to make a dress for
Beth's doll.

"She has enough dresses," Beth said. "She needs a
hat, Louy."

"What kind of hat?" Louisa asked.

"A stylish hat. One with plumes."

Louisa good-naturedly made feathered hats for all
Beth's dolls. Mrs. Alcott sighed with relief to see
Louisa out of mischief for once. Next day their
neighbor knocked on the door.

"Mrs. Alcott, do you know what your Louisa has done now?"

Mrs. Alcott could only shake her head.

"She's been chasing my chickens all around the yard and pulling out their tail feathers! She says she needs them for her business. She says she's a doll milliner."

Louisa was in disgrace again.

The year she was fourteen she had so nearly exhausted her father's patience that he confided to his journal: "I had a 'possessed one' by my side all winter." The devil, he sorrowfully concluded, had bound Louisa's will in chains that she could not break.

Louisa suffered, too. She knew she was difficult. "People think I'm wild and queer," she wrote in her diary. She felt "dismal," "discontented," or "so cross I wish I had never been born." Growing up was not easy for Louisa. "The trials of life," she said long afterward, "began early for me."

Certainly many of those "trials" arose from the Alcott's poverty. Although Hillside was a comfortable home, they had no income to maintain it. Mr. Alcott occasionally gave a Conversation for a fee. He worked at odd jobs for his neighbors. Anna taught a class of little children in the barn for a few months. Mrs. Alcott took a feebleminded girl to board. Anything to bring in a little money! Llewellyn returned to Hillside each summer as a paying guest. None of these endeavors made much profit. Whenever the family purse *did* hold a dollar, it always seemed as if someone worse off than the Alcotts needed help.

A fugitive slave arrived under cover of darkness and stayed hidden in the secret cupboard until he found a way to Canada. He was Louisa's first pupil, and she taught him how to write using a stick of charcoal, for the pencil slipped from his fingers, heavy and stiff from field work. The Alcotts, all devoted to the cause of abolition, scraped together enough money to help the Negro on to Canada where he would be free.

Hardly had he departed when they heard of a starving family nearby. The Alcotts sent their own breakfast to them and went hungry that morning. Shortly after that, on a cold, snowy afternoon, a poor boy came begging for firewood.

"A few sticks, Miss," he said to Louisa, who answered the door. "Please. Our house is cold and my baby sister is sick."

"Come in," Louisa said to the shivering child. "Wait here. I'll ask my father."

She ran to her father's study and told him the story. "What shall I do?"

"Give half our stock," Mr. Alcott said at once, "and trust in Providence; the weather will moderate, or wood will come."

Louisa and Anna heaped the child's cart with logs and kindling and helped him pull it home. Snow fell for several days. The Alcott's own supply of wood was almost gone. Then a knock came at the door. A farmer appeared.

"I started for Boston with a load of wood to sell, but the drifts are so high I can't get through. May I unload my wood here? You needn't hurry about paying me for it."

"You see," Mrs. Alcott said, "cast your bread upon waters and it will come back to you buttered."

It was one of her favorite expressions. She often quoted it to the girls. This time it had proved true. Louisa was not quite satisfied. They had wood, but it meant another debt to add to all they already owed. She was discovering that poverty, hard to endure at any age, is almost unbearable at fourteen, at fifteen. With scarcely enough money for wood, food, and taxes, it was useless to hope for new clothes.

In mended shoes and made-over dresses Louisa and Anna went to parties where other girls wore kid slippers and fine Indian mull gowns. It was hard not to envy these happy and carefree creatures who chattered about new hats, shopping trips, and the latest patterns from *Godey's Lady's Book*, the fashion magazine.

Marmee did her best. She brightened Anna's old winter dress with a frill of lace around the neck. She dyed odd stockings to make a matching pair for Louisa. She covered a moth hole with a bit of embroidery. Even Mr. Alcott tried to help. A cousin in Boston sent a box of old clothes to the girls. Mr. Alcott spread them out on the table, measured the material, measured the girls. The cousin, unfortunately, wore a very small size. Nothing could be managed for too-tall Louisa, too-plump Anna, but Beth would have a new dress.

Mr. Alcott sketched a simple design on a piece of paper.

"How do you like this?" he asked.

Marmee made a change or two.

"Give me the scissors," Mr. Alcott said. He traced a pattern on the cloth and skillfully cut it out.

The girls sewed the seams. It was a pretty dress, but it was only one. All Marmee's loving contrivances could not give the girls clothes like their friends had, or make them forget that they were objects of charity.

When "the trials of life" were too great, Louisa had one sure refuge, her "study."

For a long time she had coaxed for a room of her own.

"I want a place where I can be alone to work, Marmee. Please!"

"You must be patient, dear," Mrs. Alcott said. "Patience gives us content, if nothing else."

"Patience!" Louisa said crossly. "I suppose I shall never have my room."

Mrs. Alcott sighed. Later she wrote one of her notes to Louisa:

Dear — . . . Be assured the little room you long for will come, if it is necessary to your peace and well-being. Till then, try to be happy with the good things you have. They are many, — more perhaps than we deserve, after our frequent complaints and discontents.

Be cheerful, my Louy, and all will be gayer for your laugh and all good and lovely things will be given to you when you deserve them . . . Mother.

Louisa tried, and, in March 1846, her wish came true and she wrote in her diary:

I have at last got the little room I have wanted so long, and am very happy about it. It does me good to be alone and Mother has made it very pretty and neat for me. My workbasket and desk are by the window, and my closet is full of dried herbs that smell very nice. The door that opens into the garden will be very pretty in summer, and I can run off to the woods when I like.

Here she could escape from the everyday world into a make-believe one of her own creation. She was an author now, and in the stories she wrote, if not in real life, she could make things happen the way she wanted.

She kept her journal. She began an *Imagination*

Book where she jotted down ideas, quotations, and bits of conversations. She invented a whole series of fables about flowers for little Ellen Emerson. Louisa still wrote poetry, too. Anna copied one of the poems into her own diary, adding loyally:

> Louisa is a beautiful girl and writes as good poetry as Lucretia Davidson. . . . I think she will write something great one of these days.

Louisa had never lost her old love for plays. The barn at Hillside, as at Hosmer Cottage, was a theater for the girls and their friends. Louisa dramatized all

their favorite fairy tales — Snow White, Bluebeard, and Cinderella, with Beth abused by her wicked sisters, Abby and Anna, until Louisa, a prince in a flowing cape, carried her off in a coach made from a real pumpkin.

As they grew older, they tried more ambitious roles. One of Louisa's favorite parts was Aspasia, the heroine of a novel about ancient Greece, written by their mother's friend, Mrs. Lydia Maria Child. Louisa discovered that the tales of Sir Walter Scott, full of dungeons, bandits, and crusades, made fine plays too.

After Mr. Alcott read aloud to the family *Martin Chuzzlewit,* by Charles Dickens, Anna and Louisa would "do" the two nurses, Betsey Prigg and Sairy Gamp, for hours, improvising conversation in their cockney accent.

One evening, in summer, shortly after Llewellyn's arrival for his annual visit, Mrs. Alcott mentioned in a casual conversation that one of her relatives had married a man named Hamilton Willis.

"Hamilton Willis!" Llewellyn said. "He's a distant cousin of my father's."

"Then we're relatives!" cried Anna.

"Real flesh-and-blood relatives," said Louisa.

"No, not blood relatives," Marmee explained, "in-law relatives, perhaps."

"Are you sure, Marmee?" Anna said. She began to work out a family tree on a piece of paper. "I wish you could be our blood relative, Llewellyn."

Louisa sat silently by for a few minutes and then she slipped off to her study.

For two days she appeared only for meals and to rush through the most urgent of her daily chores. The rest of the time she was busy at her desk, and the family could hear the scratch of her quill pen, and through the half-open door, see scribbled sheets piling up beside her.

At the end of the second day she came to the supper table full of excitement, her hazel eyes dancing, to announce, "I've written a play! A real play!"

"What's it about, Louy?"

"About us ... and Llewellyn. I made it all up myself. It's called 'The Long Lost Cousin.'"

"With parts for us all?" Anna asked.

"Good parts," Louisa said.

Rehearsals started the next day. Louisa — author, star, director, and production manager all in one — was everywhere at once, answering questions and giving orders.

"What shall we do about the flag we run up in the last act?" Beth asked.

"Borrow one."

"I tried, Louy. I can't get one anywhere."

"Make one."

"From what?"

Louisa rummaged through Aunt Dolly's trunk. The

contents had diminished over the years, but she came up with a handful of clothes.

"Here, make the stripes out of these red flannel drawers and this piece of white petticoat. The blue collar will be enough for the field."

"What about the stars?"

"Oh, I'll cut them from what's left of the white petticoat."

"Louy . . ." This time it was Anna. "I can't go off the stage and come on in another costume in three minutes."

"Then I'll rewrite that scene." Louisa made a note.

The news spread. Soon all of the Alcott's friends knew that Louisa had written a real play, an original play, and they were eager to see it.

"The barn won't hold all the people who want to come," Llewellyn reported.

"Then we'll give it outdoors," Louisa said.

"How about a curtain?" Beth asked.

"And dressing rooms," Anna added. "I have all those changes of costumes."

"We'll hang the curtain between the two apple trees," Louisa said, "and put a screen at the side and come on and off stage from the barn. Now let's go over the second act again."

On a summer night "The Long-Lost Cousin" was presented to as distinguished an audience, perhaps, as ever attended any theater in the United States. The Alcotts, the Hawthornes, Henry Thoreau, the Emersons, and a score of their neighbors watched Louisa's drama unfold. Their laughter at her funny lines, their silence in the moments of suspense, the startled murmurs at the denouement scene, the ringing applause when the curtain fell filled Louisa with a new joy and a confidence in herself.

"Wild and queer" she might be, but the characters she created, the words she gave them to say commanded the attention and respect even of Mr. Emerson in the middle row, who had clapped his hands when the author took her bow.

No miracle occurred. Louisa did not reform overnight, but with self-assurance came self-control. Slowly she learned to curb her quick tongue and think before she acted.

Early in the spring of 1848, Anna went to Boston to help care for the small children of a cousin. A few weeks later some friends invited Mrs. Alcott and Abby to spend the summer in New Hampshire.

"Go, Marmee," Louisa said. "Do go."

Mrs. Alcott, overworked, worried as always about money, and in poor health, badly needed a rest. She shook her head.

"Who would take care of Beth, keep your father company, do the housework?"

"I will. After all, I'm fifteen," Louisa reminded her mother. "I promise I'll take care of everything."

Finally Mrs. Alcott was persuaded to go. Louisa kept her word. She cooked and cleaned and washed. She was patient with Beth and obedient to her father. The "possessed one" had grown up to be, as her father later called her, "duty's faithful child."

Mrs. Alcott came home at the summer's end full of new health and energy. Through a friend she was offered a position that paid six hundred dollars a year, an excellent salary in those days. A Boston charitable society wanted to employ a dependable, experienced woman to dispense their contributions wisely among the sick and needy. Here was a worthwhile task, one particularly suited to Mrs. Alcott's heart and mind. She wanted to accept, but she must, of course, live in Boston.

The family talked it over together. Leave Concord? Leave Hillside and all the hard work and high hopes that made it? Leave their friends? Impossible!

Yet in Boston Mrs. Alcott would have a regular salary; Mr. Alcott greater opportunity for his Conversations; Anna, perhaps Louisa, might teach. The prospect of having ready cash in hand, of being independent, of paying long-overdue bills, made them decide to go.

Louisa threw on an old red shawl and went for a last brisk run over the hill to one of her favorite retreats, a cartwheel, half hidden in the grass under a locust tree. Perched on the hub, she looked out at the leafless trees and sere fields. The November landscape might be dull, but her spirits were not.

She was thinking of the future — of Boston. Things would be different there, she knew. She could work, earn money. Her hope and courage rose.

"I *will* do something," she said aloud. "I don't care what — teach, sew, act, write — anything to help the family."

As if to mock her a crow cawed dismally from a nearby fence post. She shook her fist at the bird. "I'll be rich and famous and happy before I die, see if I won't!"

Two WEEKS before Louisa's sixteenth birthday, the Alcotts moved from Concord to a small house on Dedham Street, in Boston. "Not a tree in sight and only the back yard to play in," Louisa complained. She found this busy, crowded, dirty city of more than a hundred thousand very unlike the town she remembered from her childhood.

Now it was full of girls and young men from the country, attracted by the prospect of earning higher wages in a store or factory than on the farm. Waves of immigrants, too, escaping the famines in Ireland and troubled times in Europe, were arriving on every ship. Instead of the "streets of gold" these newcomers expected to see, they found only narrow slum alleys full of filth and rubbish. There, in dark, airless rooms, in cellars and garrets, families lived, crowded together, some in hopeless misery — cold, hungry, sick, and lonely.

There were kind, generous people in Boston who tried to help these unfortunates, but it soon became obvious that random gifts — a blanket, a basket of groceries, clothes, a few coins here and there — did little good. Mrs. Alcott was engaged by a charitable society to work out some organized system for aiding the poor.

As a first step, she established a "relief room," where she could receive and distribute donations of food, clothing, furniture, and money. Further, she decided, she would visit the homes of those who applied for relief to see exactly how she could help best in each case.

Mr. Alcott, meantime, rented a small room next to a book shop kept by the Alcotts' old friend, Miss Elizabeth Peabody. He put a notice in the newspaper:

> Mr. Alcott proposes to open on Saturday evening, Dec. 9th . . . a Course of Seven Conversations on Man — his History, Resources and Expectations.
>
> Tickets admitting a lady and gentleman, $5.00

"If ten couples come," Anna said hopefully, "that would be $50!" She was earning a small sum herself, teaching a primary class. Beth and Abby still went to school.

Someone had to keep house. Louisa was the obvious candidate. Every morning she watched the others go off down the street, leaving her at home. Her mother always paused just before she turned the corner to wave to Louisa, who saluted back with a duster. Then she went back to the gloomy basement kitchen, to cook, wash, iron, scour knives — to work that never ended. All she could see of the world was a procession of muddy boots passing the window above her head.

"I feel like a caged seagull," she said.

She missed the country. The Common, where as a child she had loved to wander, was not a wilderness any more, but a park. She wrote in her journal:

Since coming to the city I don't seem to have thought much, for the bustle and dirt and change send all lovely images and restful feeling away. Among my hills and woods I had fine free times alone, and though my thoughts were silly, I daresay, they helped to keep me happy and good.

There were museums, theaters, lecture halls, libraries, shops full of pretty clothes, not many blocks away.

"But what's the use of looking," Louisa complained to Anna, "when we have no money to buy any of the splendors before us."

"Then we must make our own amusements," Anna said.

So, as soon as supper was over, the kitchen became a theater. The girls wrote, dressed, and acted a series of remarkable plays. Beth, now thirteen, could paint scenery and help make the properties — a harp, a castle gate, a waterfall. Abby, eight, was old enough to run the thunder and wind machine, pour the waterfall, and draw the curtains.

Louisa and Anna took four or five parts each and made lightning changes from a fairy queen to a murderer in chains to a prince in armor. They grew adept at improvising dialogue and inventing business to cover long waits.

They did Shakespeare, with Louisa glaring and stalking as Hamlet. Dickens was still a great family favorite, and Louisa never tired of playing Sairey Gamp to Anna's Betsey Prigg.

"And whom may you be?"

"Sairey Gamp. Gamp's my name and Gamp's my nature."

"A pleasure to make your acquaintance. Will you take tea? The kettle's biling."

"Thank you kindly, and I'll try one of those delicious cowcumber sandwiches."

Mrs. Alcott's relative, Dr. Windship, always asked them to do the nurses for him. He was a frequent visitor and he had long been one of the mainstays of the family. "He comes," Anna once said, "not shouting, 'Now I will do good to the poor,' but like Santa Claus." Dr. Windship shared Louisa's love for the theater. He often rode in from Roxbury where he lived, and carried her off to a play at the Boston, or Howard's Athenaeum, or the Museum, which had a hundred-foot entrance hall filled with wax statuary and a stuffed elephant.

Any theater, ornate or simple, delighted Louisa. She sat entranced as the seats filled, the gas lights in the great, luminous pearl globes dimmed, and, in a breathless hush, the curtain rose on some of the greatest actors of the day in their favorite roles. She saw Edwin Booth as Richard III, LaGrange as Norma, Mrs. Vincent in *Uncle Tom's Cabin*. (Louisa wept when she read the book. Now she wept again at the cruelty of slave owners.)

With a professional eye she watched William Warren, known as the "greatest gentleman in Boston," in a series of dramatic spectacles, Aladdin, The Forty Thieves, Cinderella, and Bluebeard — the very same tales Louisa and her sisters had done in the Concord barn. If only she could be there on the stage! She wrote in her journal:

> Anna wants to be an actress, and so do I. We could make plenty of money perhaps and it is a very gay life. Mother says we are too young and must wait. I like tragic plays and shall be a Siddons if I can.

Meantime she neglected her journal for weeks at a time to write melodramas in which noble captives languished in dungeons, gallant knights fought duels, fierce bandits waylaid travelers. "I like lurid tales," she admitted to Anna.

The Alcotts' first year in Boston passed.

Mr. Alcott's course of Conversations had not attracted as many subscribers as he had hoped, but he was not discouraged. He began to write a book on philosophy and this occupied the greatest part of his time for many months. Mrs. Alcott's work was going well.

The poor discovered the Relief Room almost at once and came to the door at all hours of the day and night, seeking help. Mrs. Alcott dispensed food, soap, clothes, fuel orders, medicine, money, advice, and the most valuable commodity of all, her love and sympathy.

She started evening classes and, with help from Anna and Louisa, taught women to sew, read, and write. At Christmas she had a party in her parlor for forty children. A rich woman supplied the funds, and the Alcott girls trimmed the tree with bright candies and little wax candles in scalloped tin holders. There were flowers and fruits and jokes, and, of course, entertainment supplied by Louisa and her sisters.

The Alcotts' house, as well as the Relief Room, inevitably became a haven for abandoned children, destitute girls, wandering old grandmothers, who stayed until something could be done for them. One hot day, early in the summer of 1850, a family of newly arrived immigrants came to the door. Their story was one Mrs.

Alcott heard very often. The friends and the work these newcomers had counted on had vanished. They had neither food nor money. Mrs. Alcott gave them lunch in the yard. The younger children ate ravenously, not uttering a sound, but the baby, feverish and restless, cried. Mrs. Alcott held the little one in her arms while the tired mother drank some tea. That afternoon the family went on their way again.

Three days later Mrs. Alcott, too, felt feverish and restless. She looked in the mirror. A rash covered her face. She knew only too well what caused it.

She called Anna and Louisa.

"Girls, do you remember the little baby who was here?"

"Yes. It cried so."

"The baby was ill and I caught the infection, a fever."

"What kind of fever, Marmee?"

"Smallpox, I fear."

The name was enough to fill their hearts with terror. Smallpox was the most dreaded of all diseases. Those who did not die were often left disfigured, their faces pitted with deep scars, or, even worse, blinded.

"What shall we do, Marmee?"

"Try to manage as best we can. Smallpox is highly contagious. No one who comes into the house will be allowed to leave for many weeks."

"But we must call a doctor," Anna said.

Mrs. Alcott shook her head. "There is no cure, no medicine. The disease must run its course. I may have it in a light form, and perhaps the rest of you are immune."

A few days later Mr. Alcott fell ill, and then Beth and Abby.

Through the hot summer days Anna and Louisa nursed the invalids, fanning their mother, bringing cool compresses for Mr. Alcott's head, trying to make some dainty pudding or broth that would tempt the appetite of the girls. For weeks they were completely alone. Their relatives were out of town and the neighbors dared not venture close. Eventually, just as Mrs. Alcott's strength returned, Louisa and Anna succumbed. Somehow the family survived. The older girls had relatively light cases, and slowly they all recovered.

No one, fortunately, was scarred or blinded, but Anna's hearing seemed affected. She went to the country to the home of a relative where she could work and recuperate. Louisa took charge of her class of twenty children. She was almost eighteen. If she ever intended to be "rich and famous," it was time to begin.

Mrs. Alcott, of course, had given up her work for the Friendly Society while she was ill. Now she determined to help the poor in another way. She would open an employment agency for women.

Among her clients was a distinguished gentleman who came to her office early in the summer of 1851. He was seeking someone willing to perform a few light duties in the house for his invalid sister.

"I had no one to suggest," Mrs. Alcott told her family that evening. "He wants a companion rather than a servant."

"How much will he pay?" Louisa asked.

"No exact sum was mentioned," Mrs. Alcott said, "but he assured me it would be a generous amount."

"I'll go," Louisa said. The school term was over.

When she arrived, she found that she was expected to nurse and entertain a sick woman, carry all the water from the well, chop wood, polish the stoves, and sift the ashes.

"Is that *all?*" Louisa asked.

"You will, of course, clean my shoes," her employer said.

She endured it for two months and then she announced she was leaving and wanted her pay. She received four dollars — fifty cents for each week of hard work. She treated herself to the luxury of a grand gesture, one she could ill afford. She gave the money back and went home.

The Alcotts moved to larger quarters and took Llewellyn Willis and a young relative, both Harvard students, as boarders. Anna went to Syracuse, New York, to teach. Abby was still in school. Beth, quiet and gentle as ever, served her time in the basement kitchen. The smallpox attack had left her rather frail. She clung to home.

That winter, Louisa taught a dozen pupils in the front parlor. She managed to earn a little more money by sewing in the evenings. During vacations she did housework and washing for a relative for two dollars a week.

She wrote in her diary:

Summer distasteful and lonely; winter, tiresome with school and people I didn't like . . . it's hard to be cheerful when I think how poor we are,

how much worry it is to live, and how many
things I long to do I never can.

Nothing pleased her. She was dissatisfied with herself, her behavior, her "unruly tongue," her appearance. She looked in the mirror. Her long chestnut
hair and the shape of her nose were good, but she
longed for "wide-open" eyes. She went around with a
fixed stare to stretch them.

"What ails you, Louy?" Llewellyn asked.

"How do I look?"

"Insane," said Llewellyn with brotherly frankness.

She was nineteen, but she could still run. She chased him around the parlor and through the house.

Despite his teasing, Llewellyn admired Louisa. He did not find her moody or dull. "Her vivacity, her wit, are as sparkling as a brook and as continuous as its flow," he told his friends. He thought the pieces she wrote were excellent.

"You could sell them, Lu. You have a brilliant style."

Louisa looked to see if she were being teased again.

"I mean it," Llewellyn said. "Give me one of your stories. I'll sell it."

"I haven't written anything new. Now that my work-

ing days have begun, I have no quiet to think or work."

"Then give me an old story."

She rummaged through her desk. "Here's something. I wrote it in Concord — but nobody will buy it — it's great rubbish."

A few weeks later Anna came home on a visit. When the family gathered around the table after supper, Louisa casually picked up a magazine called *The Olive Branch*.

"Shall I read aloud?"

"If you like," Mrs. Alcott said.

"Find a good story, Lu." Anna looked up from her sewing.

"Let's see . . ." Louisa riffled through the pages. "Here's a thing called 'The Prince and the Fairy.' " She began to read.

"Oh, I liked that!" Beth said when Louisa finished. Mr. Alcott smiled in agreement.

"I thought it was delightful, especially that description of the Prince," Anna said. "I could just see him."

"Who wrote the story?" Mrs. Alcott asked.

"I did," Louisa said, "and I was paid five dollars for it." She opened her hand. In her palm lay a gleaming gold piece. "Llewellyn sold it for me."

Now she set to work in earnest. "I want more fives," she wrote to Anna, now back in Syracuse, "and I mean to have them, too."

The garret was her study. There, for the next two

years, she spent every hour she could spare, dashing off poems, sketches, stories, and plays.

"If only you didn't have to keep on teaching, Lu, and sewing," Beth sighed.

"But I do," Louisa said. "Never mind. I get ideas for plots as I hem."

Most of the manuscripts she hopefully sent out were rejected, but every now and then came a glorious day when she could shout, "It's accepted!" and add two, five, perhaps even ten dollars extra to the family purse.

Every penny Louisa and Anna earned was needed to help support the family. Mrs. Alcott's employment agency had not succeeded. The book Mr. Alcott started with great enthusiasm was unfinished. At the suggestion of some friends he decided to go on a lecture tour through some adjoining states. Late in the fall of 1853, he set off. In her journal Louisa described his return on a night the following February:

> We were waked by hearing the bell. Mother flew down, crying "My husband." We rushed after, and five white figures embraced the half-frozen wanderer who came in hungry, tired, cold and disappointed, but smiling bravely and as serene as ever. We fed and warmed and brooded over him, longing to ask if he had made any money, but no one did till little May said, "Well, did people pay you?" Then, with a queer look, he opened his pocketbook and showed one

dollar, saying with a smile that made our hearts fill, "Only that! My overcoat was stolen, and I had to buy a shawl. Many promises were not kept, and travelling is costly; but I have opened the way and another year I shall do better."

I shall never forget how beautifully Mother answered him, though the dear, hopeful soul had built much on his success; but with a beaming face she kissed him, saying, "I call that doing *very well*. Since you are safely home, dear, we don't ask anything else."

Louisa wanted more. At seventeen, she had written in her journal:

My dream is to have a lovely quiet home for
Marmee with no debts or troubles to burden her.
But I'm afraid she will be in heaven before I can
do it. Anna, too . . . must have a nice little home
of her own some day as we often plan. But waiting is so hard.

Waiting was also useless. Now that Louisa was
twenty-one, she knew that only work could make her
dreams come true. Back to her garret she went to try
again to write something saleable. Munching an apple,
she sorted through her papers. Stories didn't bring
much — perhaps a book? She came to the Flower
Fables she had made up in Concord to amuse little
Ellen Emerson.

She read them over. They might do, she thought.
She took them to a publisher. He was not too enthusi-
astic, but he agreed to print the collection.

On Christmas Day, 1854, she had a real present for
her mother, a book so bright and new that its crisp
pages still held the delicious fragrance of printer's ink
and binder's glue. On its cover, spelled out in gilt letters for all the world to see, was *Flower Fables* by
Louisa May Alcott.

With her book she gave her mother a letter:

Dear Mother, Into your Christmas stocking I
have put my "first born," knowing that you will

accept it with all its faults (for grandmothers are always kind), and look upon it merely as an earnest of what I may yet do; for with so much to cheer me on, I hope to pass in time from fairies and fables to men and realities.

Whatever beauty or poetry is to be found in my little book is owing to your interest in and encouragement of all my efforts from first to the last; and if I ever do anything to be proud of, my greatest happiness will be that I can thank you for that, as I may do for all the good there is in me; and I shall be content to write if it gives you pleasure.

I am ever your loving daughter,

Louy

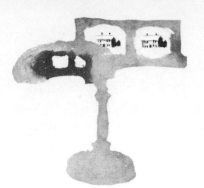

7

Orchard House

1855–1865

Flower Fables did not make Louisa rich. Her total profit on the book was only thirty-two dollars. It did, however, bring her some fame. Editors began to ask her for contributions and to pay her higher rates for her work. A theater manager promised to produce a comedy she had written.

In July 1855, the Alcotts moved again, this time to Walpole, New Hampshire, where a relative offered them a house rent-free.

Louisa liked the little town. She wrote in her journal:

> Lovely place, high among the hills . . . Busy and happy times as we settle in the little house in the lane nearby my dear ravine — plays, picnics, pleasant people and good neighbors.

The Alcott girls joined a group interested in amateur theatricals. Beth, at twenty, was still rather shy, but she could be coaxed into playing small parts. May (as Abby now preferred to be called), although only fifteen, already showed unusual talent as an artist. She was drafted to paint scenery and design costumes; Anna, with her blue eyes, golden hair, and what Llewellyn Willis described as "a clematis-and-wildrose complexion," made an ideal heroine. Louisa delighted in character parts; comic roles, she felt, particularly suited her style.

When the little company gave a drama called *The Jacobites*, Louisa, as the Widow Pottle, an ignorant, talkative innkeeper, developed her part so well that she scored a triumph on opening night. The performance drew an audience of one hundred and was favorably reviewed in the Boston papers.

Louisa and Anna still loved the theater, but their old dream that one day they might act professionally was over. It was obvious to them both that they must find a more practical way to earn a living. Anna somewhat reluctantly accepted a position as teacher in a school for retarded children in Syracuse, New York.

"What can *I* do?" Louisa asked. "There's nothing in Walpole."

"Not now, but perhaps if you waited . . ." Anna said.

"I was born with a boy's spirit under my bib and tucker. I *can't wait* when *I can work!*"

"What *will* you do?"

"Go to Boston," Louisa said. "There I know I can support myself and help the family."

"But how, Louy?"

"I'll find a way. I can sew and my play *may* come

out, and I'm almost sure I can governess some little girl."

"But where will you live?"

"Remember Marmee's friend, Mrs. Reed?"

"Where we used to go years and years ago — and ride on the rockinghorse . . ."

"Yes. She has a boardinghouse. I wrote to her. She'll give me an attic room . . ."

"Oh, Louy — a garret?"

"Not a garret, a 'sky parlor' for three dollars a week, with a fire and my meals. I can sew for her, too."

The Alcotts' Walpole neighbors were shocked when they heard Louisa's plan. Well-bred young ladies in those days did not leave their family home and go off to live alone in another city.

"How can her mother allow such behavior?" one neighbor asked another.

"A girl, only twenty-two, alone in a city like Boston! My, my!"

"And she thinks she can support herself! Nonsense!"

"If I were her father, I'd forbid it."

Mr. Alcott was away on another lecture tour, but Mrs. Alcott, knowing he shared her confidence in Louisa, ignored the gossip and gave her consent.

Beth and May helped Louisa make ready. It did not take long. Her wardrobe was small — a few made-over dresses and an old bonnet retrimmed with new ribbon. Long afterward Louisa described her departure:

I don't often pray in words, but when I set out that day with all my wordly goods in that little old trunk, my own earnings ($25) in my pocket, and much hope and resolution in my soul, my heart was very full, and I said to the Lord, "Help us all, and keep us for one another," as I never said it before, while I looked back at the dear faces watching me, so full of love and hope and faith.

Louisa found the "sky parlor" "very cosy." She described it later in *Little Women*. ". . . There is a stove in it and a nice table in a sunny window so I can sit here and write whenever I like. A fine view and a church tower opposite . . ."

After some disappointments, she found three children to tutor. She had plenty of sewing to do, and editors were buying her stories. She earned enough to pay her board and room and send some presents home. She described them in a letter to Anna in Syracuse:

I got a crimson ribbon for a bonnet for May, and I took my straw and fixed it nicely with some little duds I had. Her old one has haunted me all winter, and I want her to look neat. She is so graceful and pretty and loves beauty so much, it is hard for her to be poor and wear other people's ugly things. You and I have learned not to mind much, but when I think of her I long to dash out and buy the finest hat the limited sum of ten dollars can procure. She says so sweetly in one of her letters: "It is hard sometimes to see other people have so many nice things and I so few; but I try not to be envious, but contented with my poor clothes and cheerful about it" . . . For our good little Betty, who is wearing all the old gowns we left, I shall soon be able to buy a new one and send it with my blessings to the cheerful saint. She writes me the funniest notes, and tries to keep the old folks warm and make the lonely house in the snowbanks cosey and bright.

To Father I shall send new neckties and some paper; then he will be happy and can keep on with the beloved diaries though the heavens fall.

She went to lectures and concerts and took a course in Italian literature. She called at the theater to see if there were any plans for what she now called her "everlasting play which is always coming out but never does."

Mr. Barry, the manager, could set no date for its appearance, but he did take her all around the great new building and gave her a pass that would admit her free whenever she wished. This was such richness she didn't care if her play never appeared. She danced a jig on the empty stage and went home full of joy.

On Sundays, Louisa attended the church where her old friend, the Reverend Theodore Parker preached.

He invited her to Sunday evening gatherings at his house. There she met many famous abolitionists. Some, like William Lloyd Garrison, the fiery editor of *The Liberator*, Elizabeth Peabody, Lydia Maria Child, the writer, and Parker Pillsbury, she had known since childhood. Excitement ran high that winter. Congressman Sumner from Boston, a pro-abolitionist, had been severely beaten on the floor of the House of Representatives by a Southern colleague. It was beginning to seem that the question of slavery could only be resolved through violence. Reason and compromise were useless.

"Slaveholders will never relinquish their human property," Garrison said, "short of war." Many people were coming to agree with him.

In June 1856, Louisa went to Walpole. It was not a happy homecoming. She wrote in her journal:

Home, to find dear Betty very ill with scarlet fever caught from some poor children Mother nursed when they fell sick, living over a cellar where pigs had been kept. The landlord (a deacon) would not clean the place till Mother threatened to sue him for allowing a nuisance. Too late to save two of the poor babies or Lizzie and May from fever. An anxious time. I nursed, did housework, and wrote a story a month through the summer.

May was soon well, and by fall Beth, too, seemed on the road to recovery, and Louisa returned to Boston. May came with her to attend art school and live with Aunt Bond, who so often before had helped the Alcotts.

Louisa was soon hard at work again — teaching, sewing, and writing. She sent her father a letter on the birthday they shared, her twenty-fourth, his fifty-seventh, saying:

> I am very well and very happy. Things go smoothly, and I think I shall come out right and prove that though an *Alcott*, I *can* support myself.

From her cousin Louisa Windship she received a cloak and a silk dress, the first new one she had ever owned. She and May went to parties together. The young men they met there laughed and joked with Louisa and teased her about being a famous authoress, but it was May they asked to dance and escorted in to supper. For May, at seventeen, was a beauty, tall and slender, with fair skin, blue eyes, golden curls, and more poise and social grace than any of her sisters. If she were sometimes "childishly tyrannical" (as Llewellyn Willis said), it did not affect her popularity.

Louisa was not envious. She liked to go to parties, to see May "be a favorite," to sit in large, fine rooms, but she was soon ready to go back to her sky parlor and her work. "I love luxury," she wrote in her diary, "but freedom and independence better."

In June 1857, when Louisa and May returned to Walpole, they found Beth very frail. She had never fully recovered from the scarlet fever attack of the previous year. Some weeks at the seashore helped her, but it was easy to see that another long, cold, lonely winter in New Hampshire must be avoided at all costs. The family decided to move back to Concord. Hillside was no longer theirs. Shortly after they left Concord in 1848, Mr. Alcott had sold the property to their friend Nathaniel Hawthorne. The money received for Hillside, however, was still in trust, and with it the Alcotts

bought the house next door to their old home. Mr. Alcott set to work once more to make a ruin habitable. The family rented part of a house nearby until the work was completed.

The move did not benefit Beth's health. She seemed, rather, to grow a little more tired with each passing day, but she never complained. Life went on as usual in the household. The Alcotts saw old friends and made new ones too. Among the latter was Frank Sanborn, the principal of a private school in Concord and a great admirer of Mr. Alcott. Frank Sanborn was a year older than Louisa and he shared her interest in the stage. Soon they formed an active dramatic group which met regularly in the Unitarian Church, and a "theatrical season" was in full swing. The Emersons' children — Edith, now a young lady, and her brother Edward — joined the players, as did a pleasant young man, John Pratt, who lived on a farm near town.

In the late fall Mr. Alcott set off on his annual lecture tour. Louisa, however, knew she could not return to Boston; nor did Anna go to Syracuse. Both were needed at home as long as Beth was ill.

Louisa wrote in her journal:

We settle down to our winter whatever it is to be. Lizzie seems better. We have some plays, Sanborn's school makes things lively, and we act a good deal.

Twenty-five this month. I feel my quarter of a century rather heavy on my shoulders just now. I lead two lives. One seems gay with plays, etc., the other very sad — in Betty's room; for though she wishes us to act and loves to see us get ready, the shadow is there, and Mother and I see it. Betty loves to have me with her; and I am with her at night, for Mother needs rest. Betty says she feels "strong" when I am near. So glad to be of use.

As a Christmas treat the players gave an evening of Dickens to a delighted audience. It was the last appearance of the Alcott girls for some time. Beth grew worse and the doctor told them she would not recover. Louisa wrote the sad news to her father, who canceled the remainder of his lecture engagements and came home. Anna took over the housekeeping. Louisa and her mother nursed the invalid. Through the long, sad nights Louisa sat by "the dear little shadow," keeping up the fire, bringing food and medicine at the appointed hours.

Beth read, sang quietly to herself, and looked into the fire. Sometimes, to cheer her grieving sister, she would say, "Do Sairey Gamp for me, Lu."

Louisa, with a breaking heart, acted the comic part.

"Ah, my dear young patient, allow me to introduce myself. Sairey Gamp. Gamp's my name and Gamp's my nature. I've nursed the crowned heads of Europe and I'll be obleeged, young lady, if you'll drink this cup of nice warm milk."

"Oh, Lu, I'm not thirsty."

"Lu? Who may she be? *I'm* Sairey Gamp and contented with my lot in this wale of tears. Pray take a sip of the milk, young lady. It comes from a genuine cow."

Beth, smiling, would "obleege."

Through her illness Beth had enjoyed watching the children come from school. She often dropped little things she had made for them out the window, smiling to see their surprise. But one day she put her sewing away.

"The needle is too heavy, Lu."

A week later she called her family around her. Her father took her in his arms. She looked around at her mother, at Anna and Louisa and May, and smiled with deep content. "All here," she murmured, and closed her eyes. A few days later Beth, at the age of twenty-three, was dead. They buried her in Sleepy Hollow Cemetery. Louisa wrote in her diary:

> So the first break comes, and I know what death means . . . a liberator for her, a teacher for us . . . I am glad to know she is safe from pain and age in some world where her innocent soul must be happy.

There was to be another break in the family circle. In April, Anna announced her engagement to John Pratt, whom she met in the dramatic society. Louisa liked this quiet, devoted young man, but it seemed almost as if she were losing another sister. "I must turn to Little May for my comfort."

In July, the Alcotts moved into Orchard House. Mr. Alcott had preserved the original charm of the building and added many new improvements. May decorated the walls with sketches of nymphs, heroes, and goddesses, and in Louisa's room she painted a flower panel between the windows and a symbolic "wise" owl over the fireplace.

Louisa showed little interest. She was bored with

Concord and with the house, which she derisively called "Apple Slump."

Louisa did not explain why she chose this name — perhaps she was inspired by the apple trees in the dooryard, or perhaps slump described her general feeling of depression. For, as usual, the Alcotts' house was a center of social activity and Louisa found little time to write.

She began a book; genius burned. She longed to stay at her desk in what she called her "glory coat," an old red and green opera wrap, and write and write and write. But May was going to teach in Syracuse and Louisa must help her get ready. As soon as May left, Louisa started work again. Then Marmee fell ill. Louisa corked up her inkstand and turned nurse.

When her mother recovered, Louisa went back to her desk. It was no use. Some friends arrived to spend a few weeks. Louisa must bake extra bread and make the beds. She went up in the attic and sat on the ragbag and cried. Concord was too full of interruptions.

For the next two years she went back and forth between Boston and Concord, sometimes walking the twenty miles. She might stay a week or a month in town, but sooner or later she was needed at home again, and, as "duty's faithful child," she always accepted her obligations.

She could find a market now for almost everything

she wrote — blood-and-thunder adventures she preferred to sign with a pseudonym — moral tales, poems,
and book reviews. She wanted more than this. After
reading a life of Charlotte Brontë, the author of *Jane
Eyre,* she wrote in her diary:

> Wonder if I shall ever be famous enough for peo-
> ple to care to read my story and struggles. I
> can't be a C.B. but I may do a little something
> yet.

"I'll try a story for the *Atlantic*," she told her father.
"There's ambition for you."

Although the *Atlantic Monthly* published the most
distinguished writers in America, Mr. Alcott believed
that Louisa could meet the magazine's high literary
standards.

"When your manuscript is finished," he said, "I will
take it in to the editor, Mr. Lowell."

In November 1859, Louisa wrote in her journal:

> Hurray! My story was accepted; and Lowell
> asked if it was not a translation from the Ger-
> man, it was so unlike most tales. I felt much set
> up, and my fifty dollars will be very happy
> money. People seem to think it a great, great
> thing to get into the *Atlantic;* but I've not been
> pegging away all these years in vain, and may

yet have books and publishers and a fortune of my own. Success has gone to my head, and I wander a little. Twenty-seven years old, and very happy.

The year 1860 was an exciting one for Louisa. She sold another story to the *Atlantic*. She finished a novel called *Moods* and began another called *Work*, drawn from her own experiences as a servant, teacher, and seamstress. On May twenty-third, the Alcotts' wedding anniversary, Anna and John Pratt were married. Louisa described the day in her journal:

The dear girl was married on the 23d, the same day as Mother's wedding. A lovely day; the house full of sunshine, flowers, friends, and happiness. Uncle S. J. May married them, with no fuss, but much love; and we all stood round her. She in her silver-gray silk, with lilies of the valley (John's flower) in her bosom and hair. We in gray thin stuff and roses, — sackcloth, I called it, and ashes of roses; for I mourn the loss of my Nan, and am not comforted. We have had a little feast, sent by good Mrs. Judge Shaw; then the old folks danced round the bridal pair on the lawn in the German fashion, making a pretty picture to remember, under our Revolutionary elm. Then, with tears and kisses, our dear girl, in her

little white bonnet, went happily away with her good John; and we ended our first wedding. Mr. Emerson kissed her; and I thought that honor would make even matrimony endurable, for he is the god of my idolatry, and has been for years.

Louisa, too, might have been a bride.

"I met a man on the train who wishes 'to pay his addresses' to me," she announced one night when she arrived home from Boston.

"Oh, Lu, is he handsome?" May asked.

"Very."

"How old?"

"About forty."

"Does he live in Boston?"

"No, he's a Southerner."

"Then he must be rich," May decided. "*All* Southerners are rich. What did you say to him?"

"That I didn't wish to receive his 'addresses.'"

"If he's serious, he won't believe you mean it," May said. "You'll hear from him again."

May proved right. Louisa's "adorer," as she called him, wrote her a letter. Louisa left it unanswered. He sent another. Louisa ignored that one as well. The "adorer" came to Concord. Louisa declined to see him. He refused to give up.

May, peeking through the curtain, saw him walking up and down their street.

"Lu, do come. He looks *very* rich to me."

"And handsome, Lu," Anna said, taking her turn at the window. She and John were home on a visit.

"I daresay."

"Now he's taking his hat off and gazing at our house," May reported.

"I wish he'd stop haunting our road and go home," Louisa said crossly.

"If he's rich, think of all the good you could do," Anna said.

"I have," Louisa said, "but I don't love him."

"If he has slaves, you could free them."

"I don't love him."

"But you don't know him."

"I don't want to."

"Why?"

Louisa gave no reason. Perhaps she valued her freedom and independence too highly to think of marriage. Perhaps she feared that her "adorer," like most white Southerners in 1860, saw nothing wrong in slavery. Louisa's abolitionist sentiments were stronger than ever. The Negroes *must* be freed, and at once.

"But if it means war?" Anna said, thinking of John. "War is dreadful!"

Louisa had been to see a state guard encampment. She told Anna she found the town full of soldiers, the military "fuss and feathers" an exciting sight. "I like a camp and long for a war to see how it all seems."

Anna shook her head sadly. "Oh, Lu, you haven't changed since you were a child and used to run away to watch the militia drill on Boston Common years ago. Remember?"

"Yes. And if there's a war, I'll go. I can't be a soldier and fight, but I can nurse."

In April 1861, the war came. President Lincoln called for volunteers. Soon soldiers were marching past Orchard House along the road the Minute Men had taken three generations earlier. Many of the new recruits bore the same names as those colonial farmers who defied the English king — Minot, Wheeler, Pratt, Hosmer, Ripley. Louisa watched, as boys she had known all her life went off in their new blue uniforms and jaunty caps. Some would not come home again to Concord.

Louisa wrote in her journal:

I long to be a man, but as I can't fight I will content myself with working for those who can.

She joined the other women of Concord as they sewed and knitted for the soldiers. "We are all one family in times like these," she wrote in her diary.

As winter approached, an appeal was made for material to piece into quilts for the soldiers. From the attic Mrs. Alcott brought down the few worn little dresses that had been Beth's wardrobe.

"Not *her* clothes, Marmee!" Louisa said. "You won't give these for quilts?"

"Everything is needed," Mrs. Alcott said quietly. Louisa, with tears in her eyes, carried the bundle to the workroom over the engine house.

No sooner were the quilts finished than an emergency call came for shirts. Three hundred women, Louisa among them, worked around the clock, and in two days they finished five hundred shirts.

"A few energetic women could carry on this war better than the men do," Louisa told her mother.

Each month the Concord Aid Society sent a box to the Concord boys at the front. Louisa helped pack the clothes and food and books. She wrote comic notes to tuck inside, as well as letters, jokes, even a page of local news.

She longed to do more, and, in November 1862, she wrote in her journal:

> Thirty years old. Decided to go to Washington as a nurse if I could find a place. Help needed, and I love nursing, and *must* let out my pent-up energy in some new way. Winter is always a hard and a dull time, and if I am away there is one less to feed and warm and worry over.
> I want new experiences, and am sure to get 'em if I go. So I've sent in my name, and bide my time writing tales, to leave all snug behind me, and mending up my old clothes, — for nurses don't need nice things — thank Heaven!

She was accepted, and on December 11th she left for Washington.

The army had some surgeons and a few barracks (they could hardly be called hospitals), but no real provision was made for the care of casualties. As a result, more soldiers died from wounds and disease than fell in battle, until Dorothy Dix, a valiant worker for better conditions in asylums and prisons, enlisted some devoted women to serve with her as nurses in the army hospitals.

Louisa was assigned to the Union Hospital in Georgetown, just outside the capital. The hospital, originally an old hotel, was understaffed and poorly supplied. Louisa arrived late at night, and before dawn the next morning she was on duty in the ward.

She began her new life by seeing a man die. There was no time to be shocked or sorry. She must poke up the fire, change dressings, find blankets, wash faces, sweep the floors, and distribute the rations — "salty butter, husky bread, washy coffee, potatoes, and salt beef that must have been put in pickle for the men of 1776," she wrote home.

On the morning of her third day a loud knock on her door roused her.

"They've come! They've come! Hurry up, ladies — you're wanted!"

"Who has come?" Louisa's roommate asked sleepily.

"The wounded."

"From where?"

"Fredericksburg. The great battle is over."

"Won?"

"No. Lost! Twelve thousand Northern soldiers dead or wounded. Carts bringing them in are lined up for miles. Be quick."

Louisa hurried through the littered halls, skirting coal hods, water buckets, trays, and came to her ward. Above the door the old sign in faint gold leaf still read "Ballroom."

Within she found men lying on the floor in pools of their own blood, men with only the stump of an arm or leg, men screaming with pain, and men whose voices were stilled forever. A boy was there too, a twelve-year-old drummer named Teddy. He begged Louisa to find "Kit."

"Kit carried me. He was wounded too, but he carried me all the way. Please, Miss, get Kit."

Louisa, after some inquiries, had to tell him that his friend Kit was gone. "He died at the hospital door, Teddy."

"I was heavy and he was hurt worser than we knew, and it killed him," Teddy mourned. "I didn't see him to say goodbye."

Louisa had "longed to see a war." Now she knew

it was not flags and glory, but waste and destruction. She did what she could to help the men: she washed and fed them, dressed their wounds; she sat beside the dying; she comforted the living. She wrote letters home for her patients, messages, sometimes, of fare-well; she mended their ragged uniforms. As they re-covered, she played cards with them and suggested games. She read, sang, and recited. She "did" all her old parts — Sairey Gamp and Widow Pottle and Mrs. Jarley's Wax Works — to amuse the convalescents. She listened to their stories of home and friends and family, of battles past and comrades gone.

When night came she was exhausted, but she could not sleep. Rats scurried through her room. She could not eat the hospital food, so unlike her usual vegetarian

diet. She lived mostly on apples and bread. She felt faint and dizzy. She began to cough. Scarcely a month after her arrival she was a patient herself — the diagnosis typhoid and pneumonia.

There was no place in crowded Washington to care for her. The hospital notified her family and Mr. Alcott and Anna's husband came to take her home. It was a nightmare journey — slow trains, long waits, many changes. She was weak, burning with fever, and almost unconscious when she finally arrived in Concord.

Mrs. Alcott put her to bed, and Anna came home to help nurse her. For three weeks Louisa tossed and raved in delirium. The house had no roof, she told them. A mob was coming for her. They would hang her for a witch. She struggled to escape their clutches.

"Lie still, dear," Mrs. Alcott said. "No one is coming." For a little while Louisa was quiet. Then she woke again, crying, "I've been to heaven. It's a twilight place — dark and slow. Oh, I wish I hadn't gone."

Gradually the fever abated, her dreams faded, and slowly she recovered. When she was able to get up, she saw a "queer, thin, big-eyed face in the mirror." As a result of the fever, her yard and a half of hair had fallen out.

At least she was alive and conscious.

Anna grieved, "Your beautiful hair, Louy, what will you do?"

"Never mind," she said to Marmee and May, "it's better to lose the hair outside than the wits inside. I'll wear a wig."

8

Little Women

1865–1868

THE LETTERS Louisa had sent home from Georgetown were collected in a volume, *Hospital Sketches,* which sold well. She shared her royalties with a veterans' organization that helped disabled soldiers and the widows and children of men killed in battle.

As Louisa's strength returned, she did a few short stories and rewrote her first novel, *Moods.* The characters were troubled, unhappy people and the theme serious; too serious, perhaps, for the book received a cool reception when it was published late in 1864.

Louisa was philosophical. "I'll fall back on rubbishy tales," she told Anna, "for they pay best, are written in half the time, and keep the family cozy."

Any disappointment she might have felt about *Moods* soon vanished, for early the following year one of her dearest wishes was fulfilled. Ever since her childhood, when she had run away from home to watch the ships at anchor along the wharves, Louisa had longed to travel. Now, at last her chance had come. She, Louisa, was really going to Europe. She had imagined it all — planning the clothes, packing the trunk, receiving the letters of introduction from friends to their friends abroad. Now it was happening.

In a daze of happiness she listened to the advice of experienced tourists.

"Now do, Louisa, be sure your steward puts your steamer chair on the port side."

"Steward," "port side," "steamer chair" — what exciting words!

"And remember, Louisa, if you feel seasick —"

Even *that* sounded interesting.

In July 1865, Louisa sailed for Southhampton. It was not entirely a pleasure trip — she was earning her way by caring for a young woman who was a semi-invalid. Although Miss Anna Weld, her patient, proved rather demanding, Louisa enjoyed their weeks in England.

She sent long letters home describing the places and things she knew so well from books and was at last seeing with her own eyes. Tireless, she trooped through abbeys, art galleries, historical buildings and ruins, taking notes by the pageful.

When Miss Weld decided England was too damp for her health, she and Louisa moved on to the continent. After some weeks in Germany, they settled down for two months in a small Swiss hotel near Vevey.

For Louisa this was the happiest part of the entire trip. She became great friends with one of their fellow guests, a tall, handsome, dark-eyed Pole, thirteen years her junior. His name was Ladislas Wisinewski.

"Two hiccoughs and a sneeze and you pronounce it exactly," she wrote to her mother. Louisa always called him Laurie or Laddie.

The two had many delightful walks and talks together in the chateau gardens around Vevey. They went sailing on the lake and in the evenings Ladislas played the piano for Louisa. The two had much in common. Both knew the horrors of war. Ladislas had taken part in a nationalist uprising in Poland. Both hated oppression. Ladislas was as concerned about the serfs in Russia as Louisa had been for the slaves in the South.

In November 1865, Louisa was thirty-three. She wrote home:

> On my birthday Ladislas . . . played me his sweetest airs as a present after wishing me "all good and happiness on earth, and a high place in heaven" as my reward . . . Usually I am sad on my birthday, but not this time . . . I was happy and hopeful and enjoyed everything with unusual relish.

As the winter wore on, Miss Weld grew restless again. Switzerland, she concluded, suited her health no better than England. She decided to try southern France, and Louisa, who was dependent upon her,

had to go too, much as she regretted parting with her "Laurie."

Miss Weld and Louisa spent the winter in Nice. Letters came regularly from Ladislas. He had also left Vevey and was living in Paris. He wrote that he missed Louisa. He wished they might meet soon again.

Nice was pleasant — warm, sunny, and full of flowers, but Louisa was growing bored. She found life with a nervous invalid tiresome. She missed her family. She had written nothing for months. It was time for her to go back to work. In May 1866, she left Miss Weld and started home.

En route she stopped in Paris for a reunion with Ladislas. He took her on sightseeing excursions every day. They went to the theater; they visited all the great parks and gardens; they walked and talked as companionably as they had in Vevey.

Louisa undoubtedly liked Laddie better than any other man she ever met. If he had been closer to her in age, if she had been free of family obligations, if her "freedom and independence" had not been so dear to her, perhaps their friendship might have developed into a romance. But whether for these or other reasons, it did not. At the end of two weeks Louisa bade Laddie an affectionate farewell and went on to London. After a round of visits there, she sailed for New York.

Her brother-in-law John Pratt met her at the boat. Her father was waiting at the Concord railroad station. Anna and her two little boys stood by the gate. May flew wildly around the lawn. Marmee, dear Marmee, crying with joy, opened the door of Orchard House and took Louisa in her arms. She was home.

"Happy days," Louisa wrote in her journal, "talking and enjoying one another."

There was so much to tell. Her father was receiving some long-delayed recognition. Shortly after their return to Concord he had been made Superintendent of Schools. His Conversations were attracting increasing audiences, notice *and* fees. His western lecture trips, canceled during the Civil War, had been resumed. He was in good health and spirits, and, as always, full of enthusiasm. "Ever a hoper" he had always called himself; now some of these hopes were realities.

Anna's hearing had slowly diminished since the attack of smallpox that dreadful summer sixteen years before in Boston. Now almost completely deaf, she used an ear trumpet. Apart from this she was well and happy with John and their two boys. May, as pretty and spirited as ever, gave lessons in drawing and earned fifty dollars a month. She wanted to go to Europe, she told Louisa, and study art.

Only Marmee was changed. She looked ill and, it seemed to Louisa, she had suddenly grown old and tired. Louisa's heart sank. Would she never be able to give her mother all the comforts she had promised her long ago? It seemed doubtful.

Although Mr. Alcott and May were both earning money, the family, as usual, had debts. Louisa at once took a room in Hayward Place in Boston and began to write. Up at dawn, she breakfasted on a baked apple and a dish of bread and milk, and then she went straight to her desk and set to work.

She was never at a loss for a subject. Her excellent memory, her lively imagination, provided an unending supply of material. Anecdotes, bits of overheard conversation, incidents from the past, her old plays, her war and travel experiences, the "queer tales" that

Grandfather May had told her in that long ago summer at Scituate — from any of these sources she could build a story. A rapid worker, her pen flew across sheet after sheet. In the year following her return from Europe she sold twenty-five stories and paid off some of the Alcotts' most pressing debts.

It was, no matter how hard she worked, a precarious existence. Magazines often paid late and sometimes not at all. She still wore made-over clothes, trimmed her hats out of the ragbag; once she borrowed May's brushes and painted a straw bonnet to match a dress. At last a day came when, after sending money home, her purse was almost flat. She remembered an editor who owed her a small sum. She spent the day chasing him from place to place. Night came; snow was falling. She had not found him. She was cold. She was famished.

She counted her pennies. She had just enough to buy one small squash pie. Coming out of the warm, fragrant bakery with her precious bundle, she slipped and fell on the icy walk. Her pie turned a somersault and landed upside down beside her. Tears came to her eyes. Just then a boy on a doorstep laughed. Suddenly, so did she, and felt better. She picked up the pie and went on.

When she reached home she found a new editor waiting for her.

"Miss Alcott? Indeed I am happy to meet you. May I ask if you are busy at the moment?"

"No — not at the moment."

"Splendid. Could you do one column for me of advice to young women?"

Louisa managed to nod yes.

"Splendid. I am prepared to pay you one hundred dollars, Miss Alcott, in advance."

He laid a crisp banknote on her desk, shook hands, and departed.

She was a professional now, willing and able to write to order. When, a few weeks later, Mr. Niles, a partner in the publishing firm of Roberts and Brothers, suggested she do a girls' story, she agreed. After working conscientiously for several days, however, she gave up. The whole idea bored her. Books for girls, she knew from her own reading, were usually about goody-goodies who never did anything but faint, sing hymns, and cry. No matter what happened to these silly heroines, whether their wicked guardian shut them in a dungeon or their embroidery thread tangled, all they did was weep.

If this was what made a popular "girls' book," Mr. Niles would have to look elsewhere. Louisa soon saw she had neither the patience nor the inclination to write such nonsense. She put the manuscript away and turned to other more interesting subjects.

The next year, when her father took a collection of her fairy tales to Roberts for publication, Mr. Niles looked disappointed.

"But we want a *girls'* story," he said. "Please remind Miss Louisa of her promise."

If Mr. Niles insisted, Louisa supposed she would have to oblige him. In May 1868, she set to work again. She had made up her mind about one thing, however, this was not going to be a book where everybody sobbed their way to a happy ending. She would write about real girls. It was not, she discovered, an easy task.

She noted in her journal:

> . . . I plod away, though I don't enjoy this sort of thing. Never liked girls or knew many, except my sisters; but our queer plays and experiences may prove interesting, though I doubt it.

Mr. Alcott had often called his daughters his "little women." That might make a good title for the book, Louisa thought. The story *was* about a poor family with four girls, Meg, Beth, Amy and Jo March, who were in many, although not all, ways remarkably like Anna, Beth, May and Louisa Alcott. The adventures of the March family were based on Louisa's own past. As she wrote, she remembered and described the old days in Boston when she and Anna had played *Pilgrim's Progress* up and down the stairs, their barn theaters, Aunt Dolly's trunk of clothes, parties in Concord, the budget-basket letters, their quarrels and reconciliations, Beth's illness — all this and more of the Alcotts' own story went into the book. With such a wealth of material at hand, Louisa was able to do almost a chapter a day.

Before the end of the month the book was half finished. She sent the manuscript to the publisher for his opinion. After several days had passed and she received no reply, she stopped in at Roberts and Brothers

Mr. Niles received her in his office. "Ah, yes, Miss Louisa. About your book — I have it somewhere — let me see. *Young Women* I believe you call it?"

"*Little Women*, Mr. Niles.

"*Little Women*, yes, of course. Here it is. I have read the portion you sent to us —"

"Yes, Mr. Niles?"

"To be frank, Miss Louisa, I find it dull."

"So do I," Louisa said. She rose, picked up the manuscript, and tucked it under her arm. "But I mean to work away at it just the same. Good day, Mr. Niles."

ON JULY 15, 1868, Louisa finished *Little Women* —
402 handwritten pages — and sent it off to Roberts and
Brothers.

They accepted it and Mr. Niles asked Louisa how
she preferred to be paid.

"We will, if you wish, buy the book outright," he
said, "and give you a flat sum as full payment for it at
once."

It was a tempting offer. As always, the Alcotts
needed money, and Louisa was inclined to accept.

"I would advise against this, however," Mr. Niles
continued. "In my opinion you would do better, Miss
Louisa, to retain the copyright in your own name. In
that case, you would receive a royalty of several cents
on every copy sold."

Louisa did not always agree with Mr. Niles on
literary matters, but she had complete confidence in
his integrity and his business ability. She accepted his
advice and chose the latter arrangement.

It really mattered very little to her. She was too tired
to think about anything. The book had left her exhausted. It sometimes seemed as if her bones had

never stopped aching since she had left the hospital at Georgetown.

Her mother's failing health was a constant source of anxiety to her, too. Louisa decided to spend the summer in Concord. She liked Boston better, but it was good to be home, to rest, to talk to Marmee and her father.

When, in August, proof sheets of *Little Women* came, Louisa felt encouraged.

"It reads better than I expected," she told her family. "It's simple and true, for we really lived most of it; and if it succeeds, that will be the reason why."

The summer passed pleasantly. May, now twenty-eight, was pretty and popular, and Orchard House was the center of a lively group of young people. Anna and her John and their two boys came often. Mr. and Mrs. Alcott had visitors from far and near, as always.

Every Monday night the family held a sort of "open house" for their friends. Louisa usually sat by the fireplace, knitting rapidly, an open book in her lap. When she felt well, she could be coaxed into some kind of theatricals — charades or tableaus, or "acting-out" games.

If she were in a particularly good mood, she might "do" Mrs. Jarley exhibiting her Wax Works Museum, or the lady editor previewing the work of the famous writer Rolf Walden Emerboy. (Even Mr. Emerson laughed at this joke on himself.)

Sometimes tables were set up for whist, or they played twenty questions or animal alphabet. Often, with May or Anna at the piano, the whole crowd sang together — "Juanita" or "Music in the Air," or "Rolling Home." They danced, too, cotillions and reels and old-fashioned contra-dances, while Mrs. Alcott sat smilingly by. As a girl she had gone to balls in Boston and had been considered a fine dancer. She liked to watch her daughters and their friends do the Steamboat Quickstep, the Ladies' Triumph, and the Portland Fancy up and down the room until the ancient floorboards creaked.

About ten o'clock Mr. Alcott brought in a dish of his fine, crisp apples, and Mrs. Alcott passed fresh ginger cakes. After a half hour more of conversation, the guests reluctantly departed. No one liked to leave the Alcotts.

Almost every afternoon some of May's friends came to play the fashionable new game called croquet. May liked to saunter about the lawn, swinging her mallet gracefully, but her main concern was to keep her dress neat, her curls smooth. Louisa had no such vanity. Her hair had never really grown back since her typhoid attack in the Georgetown Hospital. She still wore a partial wig. When the game grew tense, she would snatch off her false curls and hang them on a branch or a chair, and dash after her ball. Although she was nearly thirty-six years old, she could still run like a girl.

Little Women was published shortly before Christmas in 1868. Louisa was back in Boston again. She could work better there, she said.

Early in the new year she arrived unexpectedly one evening at Orchard House. Her family were sitting in the parlor, and with them was their neighbor's son, Julian Hawthorne. He never forgot the occasion.

After the first greetings were exchanged, May looked closely at her sister.

"Lu, what's the matter? You seem almost dazed."

"I think I am," Louisa said.

"Are you ill?" Marmee's voice was full of concern.

"No, I never felt better. This morning I went to see an editor in Boston. On my way home I thought I'd better stop in at Roberts and Brothers office and see how *Little Women* was doing, and . . ." she stopped and drew a deep breath, ". . . the first edition is sold out. There is a huge order from London. Reviews, notices, letters, are pouring in."

Marmee's face glowed with pride and joy.

"Oh, Lu," May jumped up, "tell more."

"And Mr. Niles was glad I had stopped in. He said, 'At this very moment I was about to send you a check, but since you are here, Miss Louisa, perhaps you would prefer cash.' "

"And what did you say?"

"I said, 'Thank you, Mr. Niles, I would prefer cash.' Look!"

There in the living room of Orchard House, Louisa reached into the bulging pockets of her old gingham skirt and pulled out handfuls of money and heaped it on the table.

Hard times for the Alcott family were over forever.

Little Women, as it was first published in 1868, was a rather short book of twenty-three chapters. It described but a single year in the life of the March family and ended with the recovery of Beth and Amy from scarlet fever, and the engagement of Meg to John Brooke.

Mr. Niles told Louisa she must write a sequel immediately. Readers everywhere were clamoring to know more about the Little Women. What happened to Beth? To Amy? To Jo? Jo was the favorite. Everyone agreed she must marry Laurie and live happily thereafter. Everyone, that is, except the author.

"I *won't* marry Jo to Laurie to please anyone," Louisa said. She wrote twenty-four chapters more about the Little Women within a few weeks. When this and the first part were published as one volume, sales mounted faster than ever, and her royalty checks grew larger and larger.

She had more money now than she could carry home in a dozen pockets. She was able to do all the things she had ever dreamed of for Marmee and her father. She bought fine new carpets, a furnace, books, clothes. She stocked the pantry with food. She rented a carriage and took Marmee for drives. She could af-

ford someone to help with the heavy work inside and out at Orchard House.

May wanted to study art. Louisa took her abroad in 1870 and sent her again in 1877. When John Pratt died suddenly, Louisa helped Anna to buy a home and to educate her boys.

Best of all, Louisa paid every penny of the Alcotts' debts — old bills, outlawed notes, long-forgotten loans — she overlooked nothing. Only the once-poor could know what pleasure she had as she went from creditor to creditor and counted out the crisp bills — five, fifty, one hundred . . .

"Is that amount correct?"

Beth's doctor, who had waited ten years for his fee, the mill, the coalyard, the store — all their accounts were cleared. She saw surprise, respect, and affection in the faces of her townspeople.

One day, in a large gathering, she glimpsed a familiar face. It was her old childhood friend from the United States Hotel. After many years abroad, she had returned to Boston. Louisa went to her and greeted her affectionately.

"I did not think you would know me," the lady said.

"Do you think we ever forgot you? Or the bandbox? Or those delicious desserts?"

She talked with her Sewall cousins about investing her money. Should she buy stocks, bonds, or mortgages? She grew used to bankers bending a deferential head toward her. Miss Alcott, with $50,000, $60,-000, $70,000, and more to come, was an important woman.

Her mail was full of invitations, requests for her autograph, for a lock of her hair, for her opinion. Strangers bowed and smiled at her in the street. She was famous.

Reporters came. When she wouldn't give them interviews, they asked questions of her nephews playing in the garden. Strangers called. Sometimes they mistook the shabby woman who opened the door for a servant. Louisa never enlightened them.

Fame imposed burdens, too, Louisa discovered. She must have her picture taken. "They are never successes," she complained. "When I don't look like a tragic muse, I look like a smoky relic of the great Boston fire."

She had letters to answer, pleas to refuse, rumors to deny, editors to receive, and more and more books to write.

After *Little Women* came *Little Men*. Fifty thousand copies were sold before publication day. When readers begged for still more about the March family, Louisa wrote *Jo's Boys*.

Novels, short stories, magazine articles, streamed from her pen. She knew she worked too hard, but somehow she couldn't stop. She was tired and often in pain. She tried a dozen doctors. Their general opinion was that the drug, calomel, used to cure her fever at Georgetown during the Civil War, had produced an inflammatory rheumatism or neuralgia.

When reviewers said that her novel, *Old-Fashioned Girl*, was "very funny," Louisa gave a wry smile.

"I wrote it," she told a friend "with my left hand in a sling, one foot up, head aching, and no voice."

Still she kept at her desk, and with each new book her audience grew. Her stories were simple ones — homely tales of everyday people living ordinary lives, but touched with a charm that gave them universal interest.

As she once wrote of her friend Thoreau, she too,

> Made one small spot a continent
> And turned to poetry Life's prose.

10

Sleepy Hollow

1877–1888

IN 1877, Marmee, for several years an invalid, died. Her last words reflected her courageous life: "A smile is as good as a prayer."

Louisa felt as if part of her had died too, but she worked on. *Eight Cousins, Rose in Bloom, Jack and Jill,* one book followed another. It was not Christmas in many homes unless there was a new title by Miss Alcott under the tree. In all, she wrote eleven novels and thirteen volumes of short stories.

Mr. Alcott had once hoped to make the world a happier place for children. Perhaps, through his daughter, he achieved his work.

Her books about imaginative, intelligent, lively children changed some old ideas about discipline and training. Homes and schools were happier places because she set a new pattern for domestic life.

Mr. Alcott lived with Anna. He still had his Conversations and made annual lecture tours to the west. Everywhere he went, he was hailed as "The Grandfather of the Little Women," a title he valued.

Louisa, when she was well, led an interesting and busy life with her friends and relatives. She supported several charities. She enjoyed lectures, books, and travel abroad. Best of all, she now had money enough to go to the theater whenever she pleased.

May, in Europe, achieved great success. Louisa rejoiced to know that her sister's paintings were praised by John Ruskin, the foremost critic of the period, and accepted for exhibition in galleries in England and France. In 1877, May married a Swiss, Ernest Nieriker, and they made their home in Paris. When her daughter was born, in 1879, the Alcotts were delighted.

A few days later Mr. Emerson came to bring them sad news. May, at thirty-nine, was dead. Louisa and Anna clung together in their grief. May, their little sister, gone. It did not seem possible. If she had ever been imperious, demanding, "childishly tyrannical," as Llewellyn said, it was forgotten now. All they remembered was the little golden-haired girl catching sunbeams in the kitchen at Hosmer Cottage.

It was May's last wish that her little daughter, Louisa May Nieriker, should come to live with the aunt whose name she bore. Lulu, as she was called, was a happy child, and she and Anna's boys found an understanding companion and ally in Louisa.

John S. Pratt, her nephew, said of her:

> People were always laughing when Aunt Lu was
> around for without trying to be entertaining she

could keep her guests and callers in an uproar. Even her everyday talk to us was bright and witty.

There wasn't a thing she couldn't do, from trimming hats to discussing philosophy, and if it would make her family happy she would do all or any of them at once. No sacrifice she could make for them could be too great.

Louisa, remembering her happy days at Scituate, bought a cottage at the beach. The children spent happy summers there. In the winter they were back and forth between Concord and Boston. No matter how busy she was, their Aunt Louisa always had time to amuse them.

In March 1888, Mr. Alcott, who had been ill, grew suddenly worse. Louisa, in her haste to visit him, went out without a wrap. She, too, had been in poor health for some time, and the exposure brought on a relapse. Mr. Alcott died on March 4. This sad knowledge was spared Louisa. She was unconscious, and, on March 6, she too was dead.

She was buried in Sleepy Hollow cemetery beside her father and mother and Beth — not far away from their friends Emerson and Thoreau.

Courage, wit, generosity, talent, humility, were all hers, and she used these gifts well. Concord neighbors, Boston friends, readers around the world, mourned a brave and noble woman who had given them great joy.

On the day of Louisa Alcott's funeral a little girl, out walking with her mother, saw the solemn procession of Louisa's mourners pass along the quiet Concord street.

"What's that for?" the child asked.

"Miss Louisa May Alcott who lived at Orchard House died."

"But not the Little Women? They didn't die?"

"No, the Little Women will still live. On and on."

INDEX

Alcott, Abby May, 48, 49, 73, 78; nature of, 94; and Louisa's plays, 114; ill with smallpox, 119; shows art talent, 129–30; ill with scarlet fever, 135; popularity of, 136, 169; as artist, 161, 178; marriage, 178; death, 178

Alcott, Anna: nature of, 14, 94; appearance, 15, 130; early childhood, 16, 17, 23–24, 26–27, 29–30; and Louisa's plays, 35, 105, 106, 114–15; childhood in Boston, 38, 39–40, 41–45; at Hosmer Cottage, 46–47, 50–54, 63–65, 66; in Concord, 52–53; life at Fruitlands, 72–74, 78; girlhood in Still River, 85, 87; and smallpox epidemic, 118–20; schoolteacher, 130; engagement, 141; marriage, 144–46; later life, 161, 169, 174

Alcott, Bronson: teacher and philosopher, 14, 19; appearance, 15–16; discipline of, 18–19; and Temple School, 19–23, 26–30; *Conversations with Children on the Gospels*, 23, 24–25, 32; vegetarian, 39–40; "Conversations," 43, 44, 98, 112, 117, 125–26; in Concord, 45; at Hosmer Cottage, 46, 50, 51–52, 56; travels to England, 62–63; forms Fruitlands colony, 65, 66–67, 70–71, 74, 83; in Still River, 84, 88–89; restores Concord farmhouse, 90–91; ill with smallpox, 119; receives recognition, 160–61; later life, 177; death, 179

Alcott, Elizabeth: nature of, 14, 94; early childhood, 16, 17, 24; and Louisa's plays, 35, 105, 106, 114, 129; childhood in Boston, 38, 39–40, 44; life at Hosmer Cottage, 50–51, 63, 66; life at Fruitlands, 72–74, 78; in Still River, 85; ill with smallpox, 119; ill with scarlet fever, 135; increasingly frail, 137, 138, 139–41; death, 141

Alcott, Junius, 63

Alcott, Louisa May: early childhood, 12–14, 16–19, 23–24, 26–31; appearance, 13, 16; nature of, 14, 19; "plays," 23, 35–36, 38, 63–65; summer in Scituate, 33–38; childhood in Boston, 38–45; growing up at Hosmer Cottage, 46–47, 49–61, 62–66; and Fruitlands colony, 67–68, 68, 70, 72–76, 77, 78–79, 79, 80–81; a young girl in Still River, 84–85, 87; a mischievous tomboy, 92, 94–98; endures poverty, 98–101; a room of her own, 101–2; author and playwright, 102–7, 114–17; keeps house for family, 107–8, 112–13; and smallpox epidemic, 118–20; first employments, 120–21, 121–22; publishes first stories, 123–25, 127–28; *Flower Fables*, 127–28; 129; seeks independence in Boston, 130–35, 136–37; returns to Concord, 137–42; audience for works grows, 142–44; *Moods*, 144, 156; rejects an admirer, 146–47; and the Civil War, 147–54; ill with typhoid and pneumonia, 154–55; *Hospital Sketches*, 156; travels to Europe, 156–60; a professional writer, 161–67; *Little Women*, 166–67, 168, 169, 172, 175; famous and successful, 171–76; *Little Men*, 175; *Jo's Boys*, 175; *Old-Fashioned Girl*, 176; *Eight Cousins*, 177; *Rose in Bloom*, 177; *Jack and Jill*, 177; later life, 177–78, 178–79; death, 179–80

Alcott, Mrs. Bronson: appearance, 15; discipline of, 18, 54, 95–96, 96–97; views on slavery, 27; as housekeeper, 43–45; at Hosmer Cottage, 50–